BUCKS THAT GOT AWAY

BUCKS THAT GOT AWAY

FROM FAILURE TO SUCCESS IN THE ART OF TRACKING

MATTHEW BRETON

Chasing Adventures LLC

Chasing Adventures LLC

PO Box 273

Derby, VT 05829

chasingadventuresllc@gmail.com

Cover Design: Dustin Dattilio

Publisher: Chasing Adventures LLC

Chasing Adventures LLC

Editor: Sam Lungren

ISBN: 978-0-9998156-0-1

1. Sports & Outdoors 2. Hunting 3. Outdoor Recreation

First Edition

Typesetting services by BOOKOW.COM

Dedicated to all those hunters daring enough to find adventure out in the woods on a deer track.

"The only real mistake is the one from which we learn nothing."
- Henry Ford

CONTENTS

FOREWORD

IN an age where access to hunting grounds is dwindling and big woods hunters find themselves competing for tracks while clustered together on accessible public lands, why would Matt Breton, deer tracker and friend, willingly record and impart his own hard-earned lessons for success onto the rest of the hunting community? The answer to this question dates back at least a couple hundred years.

Though they have never enjoyed much spotlight within textbooks of US history, a search through the sports clippings and newspaper files during the 1800s illustrates that whitetail deer once rang as important as today's National Football League throughout American society. Deer hunting, after all, played a vital role in ensuring the survivability of Native Americans, pioneering Americans, and eventually rural families who would endure the Great Depression. As America's culture matured, reasons for taking deer metamorphosed to include recreation and trophy pursuit. Stories and accomplishments about deer hunting were shared on the same newspaper pages that highlighted arts, entertainment, and famous baseball sluggers. Deer hunting continued to penetrate the American mainstream even into the 20th century. In the 1980s rural newspapers throughout Vermont, Maine and New Hampshire continued to print articles about accomplished still hunters and trackers in their respective regions. Young and unsuccessful hunters such as myself had the opportunity to pour over the printed list of men and women in the deer slayer column year after year, wishing for sake of pride and skill that our own names would somehow appear on the page after a third reading.

The social acceptance of publicizing hunter accomplishments in conventional media has since come into question, deer slayer lists in the local paper are now a thing of the past.

Once a means of survival in the purest form, aggressive deer hunting nearly resulted in herd extirpation in more than one eastern state during the 19th century. Through the efforts of politicians like Theodore Roosevelt and wildlife ecologists such as Aldo Leopold, conservation of wildlife and wilderness areas was achieved, and we continue to enjoy this chase some 100 years later. With our industrialized food nation now providing ample, although questionable, sustenance, modern hunters face the argument that we don't need to hunt for the meat. But the line between needs and choices is blurred, and most veteran trackers prefer to fill a freezer with their own venison rather than supermarket beef. And still deep down, most of us know that our desire to hunt brews from a more primal source. It is complicated to articulate with grace; we go because we are called, beckoned, or pulled. A hunger for the tracking experience connects us to the animal we love.

Matt Breton answers the calling just the same as any other serious deer tracker. But Matt's roots and ambitions set him and his writing apart from others. A self-made first-generation deer tracker, his secrets of tracking success were not fed to him by some fella named Uncle George. Matt cultivated tracking success from hard work, physical conditioning, listening, reading, and making mistakes. Enough mistakes to write a book about.

Not unlike Mr. Aldo Leopold, Matt is a conservationist at heart. A resident of Vermont, his efforts to protect wildlife and public lands access extends from his home state, to greater New England and the western mountain states. Matt volunteers and provides financial support to the Vermont Fish and Wildlife Conservation Group, Backcountry Hunters and Anglers, the Rocky Mountain Elk Foundation and the Wild Sheep Foundation. Matt's favorite T shirt boldly states "Public Land Owner" across the chest. As a sportsman and friend, Matt lives by his own code, honorable and ethical to a fault. I recall a day where he once found a heavy deer track crossing a road during mid-day. Rather than take off immediately on the track, he waited on the road for 30 minutes to ensure that he was not interrupting another hunter's game. Matt approaches everything he does with an aim for excellence and is an extremely gifted teacher when it comes time to share his knowledge.

Most of Matt's magazine articles and short story pennings subconsciously communicate a burning desire to preserve big woods hunting heritage for future outdoorsmen. He has personally embraced the concepts of conservation and wildlife ecology that our forefathers founded, with his own forward thinking. But Matt's true unbridled passion is sliding through snow covered trees with a monster deer track beneath his feet. *Bucks That Got Away* is written with the simple intention of sharing his tracking experiences with the whitetail tracking community. Matt's first book helps the novice tracker accelerate through the tracker's learning curve faster than normal. His tales are shared so that the expert, and sometimes tight-lipped tracker, can relish their own painful memories of missed opportunity, and exhilarating close range knockdowns.

May you enjoy the stories and lessons within this book as much as I have. And finally, in the spirit of conservation and generosity, pay it forward so that others may hear the calling and live the life of a deer tracker.

Friend and Co-Hunter,

Mac Ventres

PREFACE

I love the process of tracking a buck. I get lost in the moment. Everything else fades away. The trophy story unfolds in front of me. For a long time I was satisfied with simply seeing a deer bound off through the trees, thinking that someday, when I knew the secret, I'd be able to shoot that buck. As I've come to find out, if there was a secret, it was hidden right in front of me the whole time. Learn the ways of the whitetail buck and put in a ton of effort. Simple, but not easy.

I love stories, especially hunting stories. I grew up listening to the men at camp tell all sorts of tales about adventures coon hunting, trapping, fishing, chasing moose and deer. After 20 years of chasing all manner of critters through the woods, I think I'm now able to tell my own story.

Along the way, I've benefited from the interactions and support of countless people. First and foremost, a big thank-you goes out to my father, Richard, who has traveled many miles with me in the woods as my closest hunting partner. Long before we hunted as much as we do now, he taught me the value of hard work. To Lori: thank you for being an open minded non-hunter who has challenged me to think outside of my insulated viewpoints. Your love and unwavering support, when I'm home and while I'm away, make my life easy. To Ron, Mike and Ben: thank you for the many discussions and shared hunting experiences from hares to bucks to bulls; the depth of knowledge each of you possess makes mine seem shallow. To the many guys at camp, past, present and future, who have been kind enough to share your adventures and listen to mine, thank you.

Knowing that lessons learned through failure are often the ones that are best taught, I thought I'd share my tracking knowledge. I hope it helps someone bag a buck after tracking him down. In my opinion, there is no finer or more challenging way to take a whitetail. For everyone, I hope it opens a door into a style of hunting that will lead to a grand adventure, regardless of the outcome.

Matt Breton

February 19th, 2018

Echo Lake, Charleston, VT

PROLOGUE

THE buck swam the river and then crossed the road as the eastern sky began to lighten. He was tired. After chasing does for two weeks, he had eaten little and rested less. Several encounters with humans when he would have rather closed his eyes only added to his bone weary fatigue. The snowstorm that blew in yesterday hinted at winter's imminent arrival. The last couple of winters he spent mostly alone in a high country swamp with only the company of a couple of moose. Last year the coyotes found them and took down a moose calf. Mother Nature relented and spring came just in time for the old buck. It might be time to head for that part of his territory. He would decide after getting some rest.

Easing through the timber, heading uphill, the buck grabbed a bite of old man's beard off a downed spruce tree. After a few more bites he continued on his way. Steadily climbing, he heard a door slam in the distance. He was not alarmed; he heard them through the year during timber harvest, but it did make him more aware. After crossing another road, he stepped into a brook for a drink and walked in it for a ways – a maneuver that often left pursuers, human or coyote, behind.

Out of the brook and across a ridge, he kept his nose to the wind to check what was happening. His sense of smell never failed as long as there was a breeze. What it couldn't catch, his ears did. Every noise meant something. The chatter of a squirrel, the squawk of the blue jay, and the crack of a stick were all catalogued. He could easily recognize the ponderous movements of moose, the quiet, interrupted steps of his fellow deer and the steady gait of a predator. His eyes were the last piece of his detection system. With a broad field of view, he was widely aware of movement. The woods were alive with information. Let a predator get close and he would rely on his last defense: running. He preferred to lay still and let danger pass, as it had on the first day of his life when a bear unknowingly walked within 5 yards of him.

Still feeling the desire to breed, he scraped through the snow and left his scent there as he urinated, rubbing an overhead branch with his face. Invigorated, he stepped forward and flexed his neck muscles, ripping a small tree apart with his antlers. Satisfied for a moment and feeling his hunger again, he circled around, following the scent of mushrooms, finally finding them growing on the edge of a stump. Eating his fill, he then wandered a bit, looking for a good place to bed down.

Finding a blowdown just below the top of the mountain he had climbed, he looped up and laid down. He acted automatically, as he did every day to remain safe, and placed the wind at an angle where he could test it periodically as it blew from the area he couldn't see. Head up, his eyes scanned for danger from the area he couldn't smell. His ears moved to catch anything else. While chewing his cud to digest his meal, his eyes drifted shut.

A loud crack and the sound of steady footsteps woke him. The sounds of danger came from below, near where he had fed on the mushrooms. Staying still he waited, hooves gathered beneath him. The sun was now high in the sky and he had gotten some needed rest. His head moved slowly, scanning and picking up scent. Off to one edge, near where he had ascended the hill, a shape came into focus. Tall and on two legs, it was a human pursuer. This one had come further than most.

He watched and waited, knowing danger was close but that hiding was his first and best strategy. The figure crept closer. Suddenly, the buck felt a burning across his back accompanied by an explosive bang. Exploding from his hiding spot in 25-foot bounds, he heard another thunderous crash and the snow boiled beneath his feet. He made his escape by sprinting for several hundred yards. He made it into thick cover and stopped to watch behind him. Licking the top of his back, he noticed a small wound and missing hair, no worse than he'd received in many fights.

Heart calming down, another close call with a predator successfully navigated, he tested the wind. The human was still there, but the buck wouldn't let him get as close again. There were does a couple of valleys away. If he walked at a good pace he'd be there to check them by dark. No roads to cross, he'd keep tabs on the fellow behind him but go about his business.

For the buck it was another day in the woods.

For the hunter who had missed, the chase was on.

Chapter 1

GROWING UP

FRIDAY night at camp was reserved for the men of our extended family. Starting at age 5, I would spend that night with my grandmother at her house and await the arrival of my father the next day to pick me up so I too could go to camp. I'd arrive to a dinner of baked beans and venison. After eating I had to pick up the table and then my duty was to go out on the porch to fetch beer for the guys as they played cards. Eventually I climbed to the top bunk, stacked three high in the one room camp, to lay on my Uncle Ron's sleeping bag while I listened to them tell stories. I recall a lot of laughter, often a bit of ribbing, and sometimes a serious discussion while I laid there next to the ceiling in the sweltering heat of the wood stove. Like I would for many years to come, I'd climb down to my lower bunk as the men quieted down. The soft yellow glow of hissing gas lights were no match for my heavy eyelids and I would drift away thinking about the adventures of the next morning. My dreams were slightly interrupted when the fire was stoked for the night as everyone in camp found their bunks, but the dark and quiet world outside our camp made it easy to fall back to sleep.

Waking in the cold darkness the next morning to the sound of my grandfather Harley making coffee and hearing the *clink-snap* of his Zippo lighting a cigarette signaled that it was time for breakfast followed by a trip to the outhouse. Trying to dress warmly, we'd then head to the woods.

Opening weekend at our camp in Vermont became like Christmas to me. For many years that was it – just one weekend of hunting annually. But something took hold inside of me. I loved it. I dreamed of it all year.

Our family's camp tucked in the woods of the Northeast Kingdom of Vermont.

At the age of 12, I attended a state-run conservation camp at Buck Lake in Woodbury, VT. That was the first week I spent away from home. We swam, canoed, tried fly-fishing and shot an old flintlock muzzleloader, along with receiving all the requisite lessons on safety. I got my Hunter Safety card so I could buy my license. My world expanded.

That following rifle season, I graduated from walking through the woods behind my father with a BB gun to toting a single-shot .22. I also got to go to camp on Friday night. That year, I remember Ron pushing a doe out of a swamp toward my dad and me. As she came past us unaware, for the first time I raised a rifle with deadly intent at something other than a squirrel. The doe was off limits, but I tried to see antlers through that buckhorn sight. That night, sitting at the table amongst the men, I got to tell the story of seeing that doe.

My young cousins followed suit over the next decade, starting to come to camp Saturday night at age 5 and becoming full attendees at age 12, a rite of passage toward manhood in our family. We hunted together; small deer drives and pushes through the woods. Memories accumulated and the legends were retold year after year. I was pretty sure I could repeat some of my grandfather's stories word for word, yet I always asked to hear them again.

My first buck, a 119-pound 4 pointer. Shot on a small drive with Mike, Ron and Spencer not far from my grandparents' house.

Through my teenage years I broke out and started hunting with Ron and Mike on more than just the one weekend a year. Those two were instrumental for my first deer. Ron is a soft-spoken man who is sneaky in the woods. For all his quietness, he is great storyteller. A trapper and houndsman, his knowledge of what happens across the forested landscape seems limitless. He unflinchingly introduces novices to many outdoor activities from fly-fishing to duck hunting. Mike is big presence, with the grit and strength of three guys. He is a man of action who can be counted on to get things started and finished. He is a good guy to have around in any situation, especially if a brawl is about to break out or if you need to drag a deer out of the woods. Those two have shared adventures together since they were small and continue to carry on traditions they learned from their fathers. They always made hunting about the adventure and the fun we could have. I've been lucky enough to tag along.

Me, Mike and Ron after a great day of hunting snowshoe hares with beagles.

I learned a lot riding quietly between them in the truck as we looked for tracks and discussed the merits of things like scent drags at three in the morning. Being able to traipse through the woods with them deepened my love of deer hunting. There was one November day when Ron put his Subaru in the ditch and we hunted back to a cold camp for a lunch of Cheetos and slushy ginger ale. Mike eventually found us and pulled the car out. Somewhere in my college years they took me on my first trip to Pittsburg, NH to chase deer in big tracts of timber country, introducing me to a world of deer hunting away from camp. That early muzzleloader hunt ignited a fire that still burns in me for big, open country.

One year my grandfather and I both drew moose tags, so six of us had a moose hunting adventure whose tale has become mythical at camp, retold from all angles every year. Shortly after that moose hunt, I joined the U.S. Army to become a Physical Therapist and found the military life not so different from life in a hunting camp. A few years of hunting were lost, but that only strengthened the desire to return to camp.

This was our Vermont Moose Hunt in 2000. Gramp's moose had a 62-inch spread. A memorable event for all of us! Left to right: Ron, my Dad (Richard), Gramp (Harley), James, me, Mike.

I timed my leave from deployment to Iraq so that I could get back during deer season. To be able to hunt and hear the men in camp tell their tales of adventure in the woods was an anchor in a chaotic year. The scene has remained essentially unchanged across four decades; a hindquarter smoking in the yard, glowing lights, wood fire and stories. I see the next generation getting excited to come to camp. I dream now of hearing Ron's grandson Stillman tell the tale of the first doe he sees while holding a rifle in his hands, the excitement of that moment causing a tremble in his voice.

Our hunts are wider ranging now; most of us travel to hunt multiple states across several months, yet we return to a small camp tucked away in northern Vermont for at least one weekend every year. The tradition is passed in this way, stitched together with shared memories in the same way it was for our ancestors. I think a man from 20,000 years ago would probably feel most comfortable in our modern world at a deer camp. A fire, some meat and hunting stories would feel familiar to him.

I love pulling into our small camp in the Northeast Kingdom of Vermont on the night before rifle season opens. The optimism for the season runs high and the stories flow late into the night. Often Ron will weave a tale about one buck or another from a season gone by, dragging his audience along on the hunt. At some important point, he will rise to his feet, using body movement to fully demonstrate how the hunt unfolded. He'll duck under an imaginary limb, turn his head to where the buck was standing and then use his hand to demonstrate the movement of that deer as he took off. The young men of the camp audience, Dan, Jordan, Hunter, and Spencer, will be on high alert, awaiting the details, anticipating the climax of the hunt when he raises his imaginary rifle and fires the killing shot.

After much back slapping and a few questions, the conversation ebbs before someone else starts in on a tale of their own. I believe it is in this slight pause in conversation where the magic happens. All hunters, when they hear a tale of success, run through their own memories of previous hunts and recognize a failure they've committed or suddenly see something they've been missing. This is how we learn. Through experience, a thoughtful combination of our own and that of others, an endless cycle of successes layered with the backdrop of failures, we seek to improve and get better at this ancestral pursuit we call hunting.

I love tracking deer in the big woods of New England. There is something about the chase that thrills to me. You pick up the track of a white-tail buck at daylight, follow his nightly wanderings and learn the country he lives in. You see where he checked a doe group here and fed on ferns over there before climbing to his bed. If you pay attention, you'll notice where he put the wind when he bedded down and where he likes the cover to protect him. Following that buck, figuring out what he is doing and then trying to pit your skill as a predator against his as prey is a challenge for your mind and body. There is a feeling that the harder you work, the more likely you are to be successful and the greater the feeling of accomplishment when you finally do catch up to him and put your tag in his ear. The pursuit of these bucks in these big woods is also very egalitarian – no amount of money in your pocket will make it any easier getting to the top of the mountain to sneak in on him.

As with any skill, there are many lessons to learn. Each track is different and as you gain more experience, the decisions you make on the track are more likely to be correct. Should you zig or zag? Will circling help? Go fast or go slow? These are questions you learn to answer based on previous encounters. There is a lot of information available out there from some really good hunters on how they track successfully. Yet we hear very few stories of how to get there, how to bridge the gap and first become a deer tracker. At best, this is a list of common mistakes. Like anything I've done in life, failure often teaches more than success. Years have taught me that growth follows failure if I take the time to learn. Every track I took where I didn't catch up to the buck, every stalk I made where I got busted, every shot I took that missed the mark taught me a lesson. Those experiences led me down the path to where I now have some confidence in my ability to catch and kill the buck I'm tracking. Success is a byproduct of all that hard work. Does it happen every time? Certainly not, but I feel that the odds have swung my way slightly. I know I get as much joy out of a tracking down a buck as anyone out there. The hard work I've put into learning this art, such as it is, should be shared.

A tracking adventure in the making.

I have spent a lot of time in seminars, reading books and watching videos to get better at the art of tracking. All of that information helped and made the whole idea of tracking down and killing a buck possible. But the recipe for my eventual success was missing several ingredients. The first was experience. Nothing can replace time in the woods on a track. The second was failure. Without screwing it up and being outsmarted and then learning from it, there isn't improvement. So while we often try to avoid failure and ensure our success, these things ultimately stunt our long term growth. If you shoot a buck from the same stump on the same day every year, you definitely get good at exactly that, but you'll be lost in any other set of circumstances. I encourage you to seek out challenges and push yourself into uncomfortable situations that force you to expand your mind. Be thoughtful and analytical about it, but also remember to have fun out there.

This book is intended for new hunters and old, successful and unsuccessful. Stories have historically been the way we pass knowledge on to others. I hope a lesson or two that I have learned the hard way, often multiple times, will help move you forward in your own quest to track down a buck in the big woods and bring him home with you. These stories are everywhere, if you take the time to listen. The telling of your own stories might help someone else. You still will fail, as all of us do, but don't let that discourage you. Instead, think of it as an opportunity to grow and become better. I hope these stories can help you on your journey to becoming the best deer tracker you can be.

Chapter 2

CATCHING HIM IN BED

The Brook Buck

IN 2009, Dad and I headed out to northern New Hampshire during Thanksgiving week for our annual get-away. The week started warm and snowless, frustrating conditions for folks who like to track deer. Thanksgiving came and went. We were getting down to the wire but finally snow appeared in the forecast. We planned to head home on Saturday. The storm came in on Friday night, dumping about 12 inches of snow. The power was out in the morning so we gathered our gear using flashlights. A week's worth of scouting on bare ground gave us some ideas of where to start, but finding a deer track to follow immediately after a storm can be pretty tough. Regardless, hunters hunt. We headed out into the snowy forest.

The storm knocked down a number of trees so we had to cut our way into the woods. We crossed some snowed-in tracks just after daylight. Though unable to tell if it was a buck and doe or doe and fawn, we decided to follow to see what would happen. In short order, we found where the deer had holed up during the storm. With soft snow clinging to branches around us, we were able to sneak in and conclude they were a doe and fawn. With that settled we headed back to the truck. As we drove down the road around 11 a.m. in improving conditions, we saw where a buck had crossed. The knowledge that this track wasn't there on our ride in gave us an idea of how old it was. We quickly wedged the truck off the side of the road and started in.

Cutting our way down the road.

Heading up from the river, the buck had cruised along, gaining eleva-tion as he went. Knowing this was a good sign, we stayed after him. He crossed another road and thankfully no one else had taken up the track. Shortly after, we lost sign of him where he'd crossed a brook. The two of us made a circle and couldn't find his track. Another circle, slightly larger; still nothing. We stood in the road where he crossed and talked things through. Deer don't just disappear. Back in on his trail with more focus and determination, we were finally able to tell the buck was walking up the brook.

Each taking a side, we moved cautiously upstream along the brook, expecting him to leave it in short order. We could follow his movements by seeing random drips on rocks or scuffs in the snow as he skirted around hanging limbs. The buck stayed in the little brook, moving upstream – a technique that was probably effective on his more common predator, the coyote. He'd obviously pulled this trick more than once. It almost worked on us, too! Bucks do this regularly, so an experienced tracker would not have lost much time on it.

After a little more than a quarter of a mile upstream, we came to the swamp where the brook originated. The buck had moved through the swamp, eating a little and starting to meander. He then took us to the bottom of an especially steep part of the mountain and his tracks headed straight up.

Dad declared he was going to head back to the truck, as it was now 2:30 p.m. and he was nervous because the road seemed far and we were still headed away from it. I'd paid attention to the road system and knew that we had maintained a southeasterly course, with a road not far to the west on which we could return to the truck. A brief discussion did not change his mind, so we split up. I generally plan to get back to a known road by dark so I can walk safely by headlamp or moonlight.

Dad's decision was also swayed by an element of fatigue from the deep snow. Usually we don't get on a track immediately after a storm. He may have held up a little longer if we hadn't tired ourselves out tracking the doe and fawn earlier in the day – or if he had been in better shape. Seeing the steep pitch the buck had ascended in front of us was the last straw. I believe it mentally defeated him.

I remember pulling my way up using saplings as handholds, telling myself this was the last chance. Reaching the top of the small mountain, I caught my breath for a few moments then charged ahead, fighting my own nervousness about the time of day. Suddenly there was a lot of pawed up ground where the buck had fed, with his tracks crisscrossing themselves. I sorted this out and came around and over a hump on the mountain top and, seemingly out of nowhere, there he was!

Bedded 30 yards away, the buck looked at me and then turned his head away. As he gathered himself to bolt, I pulled up my rifle and put the bead on his shoulder. I took two quick shots as he laid there and then a third as he leapt away.

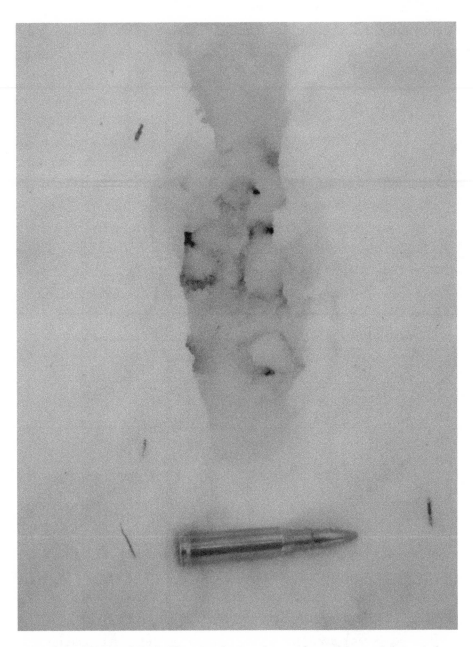

The track of The Brook Buck. Knowing the size of your rifle cartridge can help you judge tracks. Sometimes all you have from the hunt is a memory and the picture of the track.

I had always dreamed of catching a buck in his bed and thought I finally had done it. The thrill of the chase reached a fever pitch.

I walked over to his bed and saw two neat holes in the snow above the impression of his body with a lot of hair strewn about. This sign suggested I had shot over the buck, grazing his back. Not exactly what I had hoped to see.

Following his running tracks, I was able to find a spot of blood here and there. Dad finally came on the radio and asked what happened, so I briefly laid out the story for him. He headed back in my direction to help out, finding some renewed energy in the excitement of hearing my rifle shots. After our contact, I moved along on the track. Focused on the ground looking for blood, I noticed a deer take off about 100 yards away. I eventually got to that spot and saw where the buck had stood watching for his pursuer, dripping blood.

Knowing I had missed a golden opportunity, I stayed on his track, hoping to catch him again. But the light was fading. Dad caught up to me and we gave it another half hour, to no avail. We made it to the road as darkness fell, walked back to the truck making plans, then headed to our rented cabin. We booked another night, still in darkness from the storm. But we were thankful to have heat.

Back into the woods the next morning, I followed my own tracks back to the deer's and stayed on him another mile until I saw where he had crossed a road in the night. Someone else's boot tracks joined in with his. Another hunter had taken up the trail of that buck as he headed back across the river miles away from where we had started chasing him the day before. The memory of my close brush with the buck and the lessons learned were the trophy this time. That buck continues to haunt me.

Usually I sighted in on a bench rest and when that went well I considered myself a good shot. I had shot deer using a scope while I was on stand during deer drives (legal in VT). This is when other hunters are moving through the woods in your general area and as deer run off along known travel corridors, hunters on stand have a chance to shoot. This creates a situation where the deer is the one moving into my area and I have time to get properly situated. In this case though, I was hunting with a peep sight and I was the one on the move. While this can be a very effective sighting system, I did not pay attention to detail like I should have. I'd decided a front bead that was a little too low was fine, which led me to shoot a couple of inches higher than I should have. It might have been okay had I also known how to correctly shoot at a deer in his bed. This requires a lower aiming point because the buck is on his side and tilted away slightly. When you consider that half of his body was hidden by snow, it works out that a center of mass hold was at the very top of the kill zone. I've since learned that shooting downhill also elevates the point of impact above the point of aim. It is no surprise that a grazing wound was the result of all these factors. I can only imagine that the story would've ended differently had my sights been dead on.

I still wake up thinking about the Brook Buck hunt. That deer was the first one I had successfully tracked and caught in his bed. While it didn't end the way I dreamed, that miss and everything surrounding the hunt taught me things. It led me to believe that it is possible to successfully track a buck, that being in shape matters and that determination pays off in the end. As with any unsuccessful conclusion to a hunt, there was second guessing and "what if" questions asked and unanswered. But contemplating events at least allows us the chance to do better the next time. Or, if you're like me and learn things slowly, add this to the book of mistakes that might ultimately lead to success.

The Beagle Buck

My 2016 hunting season was winding down. The December blackpowder season in Vermont was my last week of deer hunting for the year. Now on the second to last day, I was on my own searching for a buck to chase.

Driving the roads in the dark on a morning that couldn't have been above ten degrees, I was able to check a couple of buck tracks. One was too close to civilization. Later, I passed on another because there was a smaller track mixed in and I didn't want to sort out the complicated weaving of tracks to start my day. I drove on to see if I could find another buck to track. An hour later, with daylight fast approaching and nothing new on the radar, I decided to head back to the mess to sort it out.

The buck track, headed downhill, was the older of the two tracks. The smaller set of prints on top headed uphill and crossed the road. I went into the woods and was able to separate things out, noticing where the buck I wanted had fed and bedded through the night. As I was following a lot of the loops and circles he had made, I heard a deer take off nearby. In the past I have screwed up by immediately chasing a deer I had jumped. Instead, I stayed calm and kept quiet, continuing to sort it all out. I eventually saw tine marks in the snow where the buck fed on a stump and a good sized bed, giving me an idea of what I was after.

With the buck's wandering unraveled I had the buck jumped up and moving solo. The chase was on. I followed him across a couple of hardwood ridges. He winded or saw me at least twice, each time starting to run after he had gone back to walking. I resisted the urge to pick up the pace. It was early and I had all day. Instead, I stayed slow and steady on the track, scanning for him. I knew that in the late season he was unlikely to go on an 8-mile cruise for does. I could hear a hound running a snowshoe hare in the distance.

Up a good hill and down the other side, the deer was feeding again on raspberry whips and mushrooms. I spotted a softwood swamp ahead of me, so I really shifted down into low gear. He crossed a big bog. I fell as I jumped the brook. Thankfully it was a quiet landing on the far side and I was dry. After a quick look around and a moment of feeling foolish, it was apparent there was no harm done. The running beagle was still bawling off in the distance. Finally, I heard the hunter shoot.

The buck crossed two deer tracks that he followed briefly. Then he encountered a third set, which he treated with the same disinterest. I snuck through a thin patch of softwood – no buck bedded where I expected it would be. I followed his tracks out into another little bog opening and across a brook that I navigated much more gracefully than the last time.

Big woods bucks often feed on mushrooms.

Looking around intently, taking one step at a time, I finally spotted a deer lying on the far edge, about 50 yards away. I snapped up the muzzleloader and peered through the scope. At 2x I couldn't tell if it was a buck or doe through the dense cover. I spun the zoom ring to 7x and I had to peek and move a little to try to get a good look. With my heart pounding loudly in my ears, I was afraid the deer would take off before I could confirm it is the buck I was after. It seemed that the deer sensed my presence and it started to get its feet under it. As it turned its head I saw antlers move. I know it's the buck I've been tracking for three hours.

Boom!

Off he goes. I took my time reloading, wanting to wait at least a half hour. Renowned Maine Guide Hal Blood recommends that wait time after you jump a deer to let him calm down. At that point, I wasn't even sure I had hit the buck. After just 15 minutes of waiting I started to get

The Beagle Buck where he fell.

cold and antsy. I snuck up to his bed and found some hair. I continued to creep along his tracks and was discouraged to see them head uphill. Mortally wounded deer usually go downhill if there is an option. After about 100 yards I came to where he fell on one side then the other and stood back up, leaving a little blood on the ground. As I was staring at the marks in the snow he took off nearby. He seemed to have a hard time going, slower than I expected. Before I could shoot he was over a hummock and out of sight. When I got to his bed I decided to give him some more time. I contemplated my options, as I had pushed this buck too early. In the distance the beagle continues to run after a hare. As I stood there, three grouse suddenly exploded from the tree above me, forcing my heart into my throat. I tried to get a sandwich into my belly as I waited but the nervous excitement almost made it difficult. After 15 minutes I decided to start after him again, expecting him to be dead.

Getting back to the truck with a buck is always a good feeling.

I sneak up the small hill he had escaped over when I see him take off. He moves along the edge of a beaver pond and I fire a shot through an opening in the small hardwood trees between us. I swab my barrel and reload again; off I go. His tracks show he returned to walking a lot quicker than he did when he was healthy that morning. His adrenaline is probably keeping him going. After crossing the upstream side of the pond, he headed into some more open hardwoods and I managed to spy him bedded 100 yards away. Using a tree for support, I shoot and he takes off again. With a quick reload I realized that I had only one shot left in reserve, plus the one now in my rifle. I quickly made my way to where he was bedded and found more hair and blood. With him wounded, going slow and hit more than once, I decided to stick tight to his track and put the pressure on. I crested over the next ridge and he jumps up at 15 yards out of a blowdown. I pull up and squeeze the trigger – click! I forgot to put on a new primer! He heads downhill and is now going really slow, so I hurry after him as I put the primer on. Within a minute, I jump him up at super close range and snap a shot off like I'm wing shooting at a grouse. Finally he's down! One more reload, with the last of my powder and bullets, I deliver the coup de grace.

The Beagle Buck. Vermont 2016 168 pounds, 8 points.

I took a few moments to immerse myself in the sensations of the hunter's paradox, the sadness and elation that come together after chasing and killing an animal you deeply respect and revere. I dressed him off and began dragging him toward the road. I know those steps are the final payments for whatever debt I incurred for this buck. I try to recall all the miles and moments it took to get to this point, knowing how lucky I was to be blessed with this buck and the season I had. Getting close to the road after a couple of hours, I hid the buck in the bushes and trotted to get to my truck. After getting him loaded up, I drove out the log road toward town and offered a wave and a nod to the hare hunter and his hound packing it up for the day.

My buddy Ben calls his muzzleloader "The Silent One" because he hasn't shot anything with it. After I got to my truck, I sent him a message that said my muzzleloader had "barked like a beagle today," with the idea of the hound I heard and the number of shots it took to get the job done fresh in my mind. A beagle never quits running. Shooting this beautiful VT buck on the second to last day of my 2016 season felt like it took a similar amount of beagle-like persistence. Even the successful hunts have lessons to be learned, like to be ready after you've shot the buck and to put a primer on your muzzleloader every time you reload!

Chapter 3

WIDE RIGHT

Binocular Buck

IN 2014, I had a season of close calls and missed opportunities. Dad and I had a buck we were tracking in NH get shot in front of us, I missed a buck in Maine during our Thanksgiving week hunt, and I hesitated on a small buck in Vermont for a split second too long. Each situation taught me more about tracking deer. I was still hard at it into Vermont's blackpowder season. This is one of the last hunting opportunities in northern New England, so despite some pretty cold temperatures, I kept grinding.

All of this came on the heels of a great 2013 that saw Dad and me have success on a grand Wyoming adventure for elk and mule deer. On that WY hunt I learned the benefit of using binoculars – we glassed a lot out there. I had become used to carrying them and I thought that they paired nicely with the peep sights I was using on my rifle and muzzleloader.

During rifle season I had tracked a good buck, crossing his path on a particular road I like to drive before first light. That buck was aggressively after the does and I spent far too much time sorting out barnyards of tracks, never gaining any ground on him. While I didn't catch up to that one, I learned the area to some degree. With some fresh snow a couple of weeks later, I decided to head in and see if I could find either that same buck or a different one to track.

I parked the truck and worked my way into the woods, paralleling a brook and heading upstream. The logging buffer along this brook created a nice edge habitat that the deer seemed to like. They had the feed bag on with the rut over and winter coming. Temperatures that day were around 0° F. I knew it wouldn't be long before the deer started to migrate toward their winter yards. Luckily the bucks generally lag behind the does on this transition, so you can often find a buck doing his own thing. I eventually cut the tracks of several deer and started to follow them as they led into a clear cut that was a couple years old. As the deer's tracks spread out in the midst of where they had fed it became apparent that there was a buck in the mix. These deer had milled around quite a lot feeding, and then seemed to get together again and move into another area. Recalling my inability to catch up to the buck a couple weeks before, I cruised through these areas, keeping tabs on the group but not trying to follow each step of the buck.

As I worked through a number of these feeding sessions, I felt like I was beginning to make up some time on these deer. I had to make a couple loops around the tracked up areas to be sure I didn't lose any members of the group but I was confident the buck was still there. Based on many previous experiences, these situations are often when I lose a track. This is especially true if the buck I am tracking is not significantly bigger than the does he's with. That was certainly the case here. After a couple hours of tracking through this feeding sign, the buck tracks finally split from the group. I missed it at first and was still following the does, but eventually I noticed his track wasn't in the mix anymore.

Typically with a group of tracks, I see the sign of the last deer in the group, with evidence of other deer popping up intermittently within the trail. So, while it can be frustrating, I try to balance the speed required to catch up to the buck against the likelihood of misplacing the track. It is not unusual to get what we call a "tracker's headache" when trying to sort out tracks like these, staring at blindingly white snow. It takes a lot of effort to stay mentally focused while tracking, but that is also part of the enjoyment.

Going back to the last known location of the buck's track, I was able to swing wide, patiently sort it out and catch where his track left the group. At this point I took a break to refocus, get some water and a bite to eat. Now I had a solitary buck to track.

I was in catch-up mode, cruising along the still-frozen tracks. It was time to get close and make something happen. The buck started to travel into some steeper country, moving up and down ridges through more softwood. After all the eating he had done and the wandering I was starting to see in his tracks, it seemed he was ready to bed. Going down one side of a ravine and crossing a brook to go up the other side, it struck me that there was no way I'd catch this buck in his bed in this type of country. It was rough going.

An empty bed during muzzleloader season.

As I topped the other side, there was his bed. Disappointed that I'd blown it, I took a minute to evaluate the situation. The bed was frozen and he'd walked away from it, meaning I didn't jump him. Things were looking up; the track was now much fresher. In short order I found some pellets that weren't frozen. Knowing the cold temperatures of the day would freeze his scat pretty quickly; this buck hadn't left too long ago.

Easing along the track, I was looking for him intently. After 45 minutes of slow stalking, I gazed across one area and when I swung back, there he was. He had the drop on me from about 40 yards away behind a small fir tree. His head was down on my first glance through and I simply missed seeing him. I wanted to get a good look, so rather than raise the muzzleloader, I slowly brought my binoculars up from underneath my left arm and confirmed it was a buck standing there, antlers as wide as his ears and brow tines as well.

I put the binoculars down, raised the muzzleloader and got the bead on him. All of this might have taken 2 or 3 seconds total, but it was enough that buck got nervous and decided to head out, right as I pulled the trigger. At first essentially standing broadside, his flight started as he rocked back onto his hind legs, then whirled around to run straight away. With the muzzleloader aimed at his shoulder before he moved, I missed wide right, right where he had been.

In the time it took to raise and lower my binoculars, I likely would have been able to shoot that standing buck if I was using a scope. Determining the right hunting equipment is an entirely individual experience and is one that evolves over time. For me, the use of a peep sight, while traditional and enjoyable, ultimately proved impractical and ineffective. This choice was made more clear one summer with some friends, shooting at a rolling tire. I used my peep sight equipped rifle for the first round and only hit the target once out of four shots. On my second turn, I used my scoped .30-06 and was able to put three rounds out of four in the tire. This made it obvious that I should just stick with a scope.

I now outfit my tracking rigs with scopes mounted on a rail with quick release rings and a peep sight for back up. If something happens to my scope or the weather is particularly foul, I have back up options available.

I gave the buck some time and took up the track again, seeing no sign of a hit. He eventually settled down and headed up the mountain. He picked his bed carefully near the top. This time he winded me before I got anywhere close enough to get another shot. With a buck on the run, headed down the other side of the range, that was the end of the road for my tracking season.

Sunrise Miss

During Thanksgiving week of 2015 Dad and I were in Maine again. With the forecast calling for a coastal storm, we made the last minute decision to travel to a new area and take advantage of the snow rather than pound bare ground in familiar country. We had a good week with snow starting on Monday that stayed around until Thursday. We got into some good buck sign and covered some new territory, so it was exciting and refreshing, but there was no buck on the game pole. With no snow around anywhere within driving distance at the end of the week, we decided to hunt closer to where we were staying. We pulled into the end of a log road before daylight, got our gear together and formulated a plan for the day.

As the sun started to come up we walked together up the blocked-off road. It meanders into the back of a clear-cut we had explored in previous seasons, so we knew we were in good country. Quietly walking up the road, all of a sudden there was a flash of tail and a good-sized body bounding to the left off into the cut. Dad hadn't seen it but I said "Deer!" and ran up to where I could look. I expected to see the deer running through the cut so I scanned into the distance. Seeing nothing, my focus was drawn back closer to me. There he was, standing 30 yards below me, the white 'V' of his tail plainly visible in the waxing daylight. I pulled up my rifle and got the deer in the scope, found its head and noticed his antlers. The bases were quite big. I got an impression of the rack over his head. I moved the crosshairs down for a shot.

Blocked logging roads can be a good place to find buck tracks.

With his body oriented away from me, the deer was looking back in my direction over his right shoulder with very little vital area exposed. I tried to sneak a bullet into those vitals, pulling the trigger as I dropped the crosshairs down. The deer leapt to his right at the shot and I led him a little as I fired the next round, but he landed short of where I anticipated and I know I missed him with that one. Cycling the action for a third shot, he was gone.

Having pushed it too early in the past, Dad and I decided to back off and give things some time. I headed back to the truck to change my boots. I had planned to walk with Dad into the back of the cut and then sit for a while. Now we were chasing a buck. Dad stayed put. I got back to the truck in about 15 minutes and heard a shot ring out. Trying to stay calm, I got my rubber boots on and headed back up.

I met with Dad and found out he had seen the buck cross the logging road. He had to take an offhand shot and said he was holding high. The shot was a long way off by New England standards; we later measured it at 280 yards.

We went back and reassessed my original shots. I got down where the buck had been and looked for sign of a hit. No hair, no blood, just running tracks from his escape. It may seem odd that buck was standing there after we spooked him. In the big woods, he more often encounters a predator who must make contact with him to cause him harm, like a coyote, so his responses are calculated for this. His departure will often be delayed if he has to figure out what is going on – when his eyes, ears or nose don't tell him something definitive.

When tracking a buck in the big woods, the shots are often less than the ideal, standing-broadside shot at a calm, unaware animal. This opens trackers up to some criticism by our stand-hunting brethren, but a rushed shot might be all you get in a week of tracking. It is paramount to use the right equipment and be prepared to execute under a wide range of conditions. Proper practice makes this situation more tenable. I spend time snap shooting and plinking at stationary skeet set up at various distances. Rolling tires with targets in the middle of them also help to be ready for running shots. Ethical shot selection is ultimately is an individual judgement. I think that picking a good shot opportunity that a hunter has trained for keeps us from waiting for the 'perfect' shot that often never happens. In describing this miss to people, I usually boil the message down: I got too cute, or picky, with the shot. I make sure that I know that I have enough gun and enough bullet to make a kill when I take the shot, whether that is broadside, facing on, dead away, quartering toward or quartering away. This is especially true on snow, when follow up can be assured. Experience and practice will allow each hunter to make a split second judgement of what to do, but for the dedicated tracker, I advocate finding a way to get a lethal bullet into the animal.

Knowing where the buck had crossed the road, Dad headed out while I worked my way into the cut. The running tracks made it easy to track this buck on the bare ground, but when he started to walk it got much harder. I eventually followed the tracks out to Dad without evidence of a hit. We found a small pile of hair where Dad's shot had connected. We followed the running tracks again, there was still no blood. Back in the woods now, it was easier to follow the walking tracks. I was able to pick things out slowly as the buck continued to head uphill. After more than an hour of this, covering less than a mile, I jumped the buck. With only a brief glimpse and no shot, I went to inspect the bed he had just exited. No blood, no hair, nothing to suggest any of our shots had done this buck any serious harm. It is easy to get distracted while on the track or even not be ready as the day starts. Run-ins with bucks can happen anywhere at any time in the big woods. The hunter who is ready will capitalize.

I suspect that the early morning encounter with us had only sidetracked the buck and he had gone uphill to bed where he had originally intended to go. I tried to stay on his track but lost it as he left the country above the cut, mixing in with other tracks. Disappointment clouded the afternoon and we found ourselves in the same area the next day. We hoped for lightning to strike twice and encounter this buck again or to discover something we might have missed, but that morning had been our chance for the week.

The Wide Right and Sunrise Miss bucks were encountered less than a year apart. These stories demonstrate some success in getting close and getting an opportunity at a buck, but both also clearly outline that simply being close doesn't finish the job. For a long time I was so concerned with catching up and seeing the buck that I hadn't really given thought to actually closing the deal. Chances at bucks in the big woods are rare; it is important to capitalize when it does happen. I plan and prepare differently now for what to do when that buck is there and I only have two seconds to make the shot. That can make the difference between eating venison and tag soup.

The Long Drive Buck

Dad and I returned home on Sunday after wrapping up the fourth week of rifle hunting in Maine. I had experienced some odd truck problems in my old Nissan while we were on our trip, so I got that checked out on Monday and then worked Tuesday through Thursday, with Friday off and the weekend ahead. There wasn't a season open in VT that week for deer, but southern New Hampshire was open for rifle hunting and Maine had its full state muzzleloader hunt that week. My work is schedule-based so I can't just take off when conditions are right. But, I've found that if I schedule a few days off per week through the season, I can often get to good snow if it comes.

Back at work, I watched the weather intently. A snow event was going to hit Maine on Thursday. Knowing that the initial storm would shut movement down, I decided to head out with plans to hunt Friday and Saturday. I woke up at 2:30 a.m. and pointed the truck east, knowing I had two days to get it done. Driving along the snowline, I made my way to the general area Dad and I had hunted the week prior – the snow wasn't going to amount to much further north where we'd each missed that buck the week before. I finally pulled into the road system around

Maine 2015 Long Drive Buck. 148 pounds and 7 points. Note how the snow is hanging on everything.

8:30 a.m. and found a few inches of good snow. I drove in looking for tracks. There was only one truck ahead of me on the road. I had a backup plan to strike off into the woods if nothing piqued my interest. I found a couple sets of different tracks. One was a buck with two does headed into a swamp. I initially left those because I would rather track a lone buck if possible. Having extra eyes and ears on alert can make things challenging from a stealth perspective. I also find tracking deer in a swamp is tough because the woods can be thick, making it hard to get close enough to see a buck. Given my late start into the woods and my desire to be on a track, I turned around and headed back to take them.

I worked my way in through the trees, trying to get in the groove, washing the road noise out of my head and settling into the woods. Twenty minutes later as I followed these three deer, I realized I had for-

Loaded up for the drive home to Vermont.

gotten to put the primer on my muzzleloader. Kicking myself, I paused to put one on, took a deep breath and carried on. The snow was new overnight and these tracks were fresh, so I didn't feel I had to hurry. After about an hour on the track, I bumped a couple of deer to my left. I froze in place and saw a different deer moving to my right, almost sneaking off with its tail down. Given how quiet and snow covered the woods were, I didn't think I had really blown them out of there. I gave one grunt on my tube and slid around a tree to look into a bigger opening. There was a deer standing about 50 yards away in raspberry whips. I pulled up my scoped muzzleloader and got a look at the deer. I saw that he had a rack as he looked back at me over his shoulder, but the angle was reminiscent of the shot I had missed just a week earlier. I pictured the kill zone hiding in front of his near side rear leg and aimed there. I pulled back the hammer and then touched off the muzzleloader. Everything was lost in a cloud of smoke.

Sneaking up to where he had stood after I reloaded, I discovered hair but no blood. There was a moment of panic. I calmed down and followed his running tracks for a bit, waiting and hoping for the blood to start. Instead I found him piled up! The entrance was in the meaty part of the hindquarter and the bullet traveled the length of him into the lungs. Not getting too picky with the shot had paid off. Pretty happy about how things went, I gutted him, dragged him a quarter mile to a road, got him in the truck and headed west toward home. I ended the day by dropping the buck off at Dad's to hang while we had a beer and I shared the story. I finally pulled back into my driveway around 10 p.m. With 550 miles staring out the windshield of my truck and being awake for more than 20 hours, I decided I wouldn't work that hard if you paid me. But to track a buck down made it worth every second.

Chapter 4

CHESS MATCH

Outwitted

A buck I tracked when I was back in college taught me a few things about tracking deer, especially deer that have been around for more than a season or two. At that time, I had experience deer hunting at home but had seldom ventured into unknown territory on my own. Near camp we usually hunted on drives or in familiar country. I had spent time trailing deer, but not seriously tracking them. As much fun as that was, I dreamt of more. Books and videos by the Benoit family had entered my life. I decided I wanted to be a deer tracker. I didn't even own a truck, but I would beat my little front-wheel-drive Ford Escort back as far as I could to chase a buck.

I was hunting near a buddy's camp along the spine of the Green Mountains that rifle season. I had gotten into some good territory. There wasn't a ton of hunting pressure there that year for some reason, so it was fun hunting. The snow also seemed to be good because there wasn't a crust and we got a little every day. The snow tended to be light but slightly sticky, so that tracks were distinct each day. I got onto what I thought were buck tracks most days, though at that time I was probably 50/50 on identifying them accurately. I cut this buck's track from the road as I headed in to where I had been hunting. Taking off on the track, it was apparent this buck was up to something different. The previous bucks I had followed consistently headed west into groups of does around a large cut. This deer headed east, taking me into some rugged country.

After crossing a second dirt road in the valley, he made his way around a couple of ponds in some rocky terrain and then to the base of a mountain. As we headed up this mountain, there were a series of benches that this buck started to angle across and up. I finally found sign of him feeding. In those days, I didn't slow down for much, so I kept driving on. Making good time, I eventually jumped the buck up and heard him crash off, only seeing a flash of his tail. Not realizing that this buck was likely tired from a night of chasing does and that the odds were good that he would want to bed down again, I stayed on him pretty aggressively. In the course of a couple hours I ended up jumping him a couple more times. I could see where he would wait and watch for me and then take off. I was only catching glimpses of him here and there as he always picked good spots to hide and definitely used the terrain to his advantage. After a few hours of this I finally had enough of being outwitted by that buck and decided I'd loop up a bench higher off his track and see if I could catch him from above.

I moseyed along that next bench, feeling pretty smug about outsmarting the buck with this move. I expected to jump him up at any moment or worst case, cut his tracks and continue up the mountain. As neither thing happened I began to seriously doubt myself. I started debating my options and began to head back downhill. When I didn't cross his track on that next bench, I was really unsure of what to do. I started moving backward a level below where I had been. Knowing he wouldn't be that far back, I dropped down another level, heading in the original direction, essentially weaving my way down these benches that the buck had taken me up.

Except now I didn't know where that buck was at all.

Drifting off the track caused me to lose information that I could have used to anticipate the whereabouts and behavior of the buck. I have tracked enough bucks to know that they have different personalities and will also behave in different ways depending on the day. Some days they

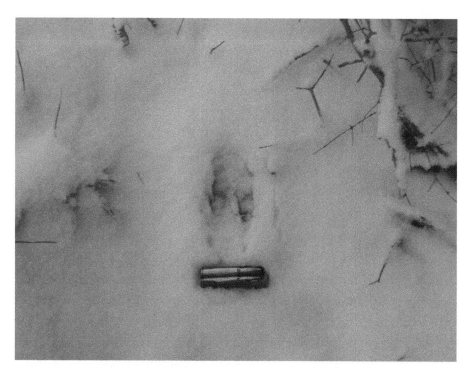

While you can't tell everything from a single track, finding one that is wide is a good start to getting in the game.

are experts in survival, some days all they can think about is the hot doe they are chasing. Splitting off the track sometimes gets the job done, but this time around it was the wrong move. The buck was giving me a variety of signs that told me he just wanted to eat and lay down. He was probably dead tired from rutting all night and was keeping just beyond arm's length. I got too far away from the track and was essentially operating blind.

At that point I had really lost my focus and, of course, that's when I jumped the buck. Being slightly above him as he took off to my left, I got a good look at his rack as he plunged down off the bench and out of sight before I could even lift my rifle. The sight of him thrilled me. That was the last straw for that buck and he was headed out of Dodge. He ran around part of the mountain and then descended quickly off a finger ridge to cross a dirt road, a river and then a town road to head into another big section of country with an even more rugged mountain to climb. I followed his tracks to the river and, being late in the day, I decided that I would walk the road back to my car.

Many mature bucks have been chased before and they know exactly how much energy to exert to stay away from a hunter. This is especially true in places that get a lot of hunting pressure. Learning how deer react to pressure in different areas will be helpful in determining how best to hunt them. Bucks that survive a season or two quickly learn to avoid humans.

It seems that two personalities develop in bucks pressured by trackers. Those bucks that are often chased by hunters who stay on them will learn to run for miles and never seem to stop, usually heading for nasty terrain. Others encounter guys who give up more quickly after spooking them and these bucks seem to learn to settle back down after a good run, but often get very sneaky. Both bucks present unique challenges and they each require something a little different to outwit them.

This buck gave me all the clues I needed to be successful. A buck that is feeding, bedding and heading uphill is one that can be killed. Unfortunately, I didn't pay attention to detail and allowed him to win the chess match that day.

Having left the track, I was walking along the road I ran into a guy who had discovered the buck's track and had followed it to the edge of the river. Without an easy way to cross in the waning daylight, I decided to head in the opposite direction toward my car and left the guy to spend the last hour of daylight crossing the river. I walked the road with my rifle slung and was surprised to get a ride from a local fellow. We talked a little deer hunting on the drive to my car. After he dropped me off, I still had some extra time thanks to the unexpected ride, so I drove out along where the buck had crossed toward that bigger mountain. I slowed to see his track and found the other hunter's boot tracks following the deer into steep terrain. Kicking myself a little, all I could think before driving off was that if this fellow has some strong legs to climb quickly, he might get a crack at that buck. But the hunter would need to be on his game to avoid being outwitted!

Two Bounds Buck

The snow was fresh for the last day of the 2011 VT muzzleloader season. I had an itch that needed to be scratched for a particular area of Vermont that was somewhat near home, but that I hadn't hunted much. I drove in before daylight. Not finding any tracks to follow from the road, I decided to head into the woods to find a track. I fully expected to cut a buck track. After finishing an early morning, five-mile swing around a big mountain bowl, I was back where I started without a track. Tracking a late season buck was my desire, but this obviously wasn't the spot to do it. Down but not out, I climbed back into the truck to figure out my next move. I decided I'd head to a different area. On the last day I felt I should really give everything I had left to make it happen. There would be about 10 months until I could get another chance to track.

I drove out the logging road and a few miles out I cut a buck track crossing uphill. I jumped out of the truck to take a look at it. It was a good-sized track, had a good step length and width of stagger – definitely a respectable buck for the area. I knew the track was fresh because I had driven in on this same road early in the morning, as had a few other vehicles, and his sign was on top of all of it. Knowing there were other hunters in the area, I hated the thought of cutting someone off so I gave it a little time before I headed into the woods. I took a few minutes and ate my lunch so I wouldn't have to carry it with me, then I tanked up on water.

I've learned to take a track whenever I find one. Starting a buck at 11 a.m. is not too late. While I obviously won't catch them all, I have been surprised with those I have caught up to and usually end up at least having a good story for the afternoon. The alternative plan for that time of day is to change areas, sit until dark, or just call it quits. None of those options really excite me. I try to play catch up while trailing a buck that

I start late, going faster than normal with a plan on spooking him. Then at least I have something to work with. A jumped buck late in the day is likely to provide only one chance to make something happen.

I moved along the relatively fresh track with only the short afternoon left on this December day. Side-hilling below some cuts, the buck fed a little during my first hour on the track and, without much warning, I bumped him out of his bed just an hour and a half into the track in the open hardwoods. Giving him some time to settle down, I took a break. I knew my chances were good with a very fresh buck track ahead of me. The only downside was that he was aware of me. I was hoping to get another crack at him. I followed his track east while most of the other deer sign was headed west toward one of the local deer yards a dozen miles away.

The winter before this hunt I had listened to a talk by two engaging Adirondack trackers, Jim Massett and Joe DiNitto, and they outlined a very specific late season strategy for tracking bucks. They used the analogy of a late season buck acting like a guy returning home from work: getting off the highway, heading for his house, his kitchen and then finally his bedroom. The thoughts of that seminar entered my mind; this buck was certainly off the highway and headed in the direction of his bedroom.

Stepping it out, the buck exited some softwood and fed heavily on mushrooms that were all over the sides of a tree trunk. The buck had just visited his kitchen. Knowing the buck had previously bedded in open hardwoods, I started scanning around for him. Seeing nothing, I snuck along, peeking ahead as much as I could. The track swung uphill along the border of a cut, taking me up through some pretty rocky terrain. As the track headed uphill, the trail went abruptly to my right and I felt like the buck would be bedded soon. Peering ahead, moving forward cautiously, I found my way to his empty bed. Damn! The finishing stalk had been blown.

Or had it?

I saw his walking tracks nearby. He had stood in his still-soft bed and then moved along the southern edge of this outcropping and fed a little more. Hearing the echo of the Adirondack Trackers in my mind, I thought the situation over. In this case, they would advocate a quiet side step, sliding along and looking for the buck with weapon to shoulder and at the ready. A nerve wracking pace; so slow, so tense. And so effective. The intensity of focus with this finishing act was something I was missing for a lot of my hunting career. Getting it right is often the difference between a blown stalk with tails bouncing through the woods and wrapping your hands around a set of antlers.

I moved along looking, looking. The minutes seemed to stretch out. My nerves were on hair trigger. Suddenly there he was, leaping out of his bed from a little depression in the earth. I don't know what gave me away, a puff of wind or a cracking stick perhaps, but the buck was suddenly on the move a mere 12 paces away. I swung the muzzleloader to my right with the first bound, moved my sights onto him on the second bound and readied myself to fire as he landed on the third. It never came. He angled below me out of sight with that bound, and then popped back into my vision headed straight away from me, directly downhill. He kept bouncing left and right through the rocky terrain and I was forever behind his movements. His rack was as wide as his body and I have the shadow of a memory that he was short-tined. Of no matter, he was gone. With my pump rifle I think I would have been able to get a shot or two at him. Being held to one shot with the muzzleloader made me hesitate to shoot at all.

The neuromuscular reflexes required to shoot a buck on the run out of his bed at close range must be almost instantaneous. A buck might hesitate now and then, but I now feel I need to be ready to shoot him on the second bound, not the third. Good practice for me during the deer season is to safely pull up on grouse when they flush and attempt to get my crosshairs on target as quickly as possible.

I stayed on that wide-racked buck for another hour or so until he crossed a different logging road and a big brook. He never slowed down.

Think about the buck you are tracking being in his bed if he heads uphill after feeding.

It was a couple of miles back to the truck and that was it, the best chance of the 2011 Vermont season on the last afternoon had simply bounded away. You don't always knock the deer down during the end game, but getting within 12 paces of a spooked deer tells me I did more right than wrong. I feel some success from this one even though I was never able to grab ahold of his antlers.

It is amazing what can be learned without even pulling the trigger. The evolution from stand hunter into a tracker is a multi-layered transition. There are old habits to lose, like waiting for a perfect wind to get in the woods or only hunting the last 90 minutes of daylight. In other cases, existing techniques, like sneaking through the woods need to be refined, so that it is done at a faster pace. A tracker needs to learn how to spot a deer while on the move before it spots you. Plus there are always new things to learn, like identifying a buck track from a doe track, recognizing sign that he has fed and is bedded nearby. All of this can be enhanced by talking to other hunters who hunt this way or by reading books and attending seminars. I heard once in physical therapy school that an expert just does the basics very, very well. The basics of deer tracking range from aging a track in old snow to learning to keep a buck's tracks sorted out from all the other deer that fed in that area last night. As learning progresses, it is vital to realize what a buck is doing and consider why he is doing it, then figure out when to go fast on a track and when to slow way, way down. The deer tracker should also be well versed in the many other aspects of being in the woods. A solid ability to navigate using map, compass and GPS is required. There should be basic woodsmanship skills and an understanding of the biology of deer and other creatures. If a tracker wants to be an expert deer hunter, he must master many skills.

Virtues like patience, persistence and discipline will be rewarded as a tracker. A thoughtful hunter who develops an approach and a system specific to tracking will experience success. All of this effort and focus should be tempered by having fun in the woods. The challenge of it all is what makes the pursuit worthwhile. Nothing that is good comes easily.

Grazer Buck

Dad and I started into the woods together, parking not far from camp on a fresh snow during the second weekend of the Vermont rifle season. Thinking we'd like to double team on a good track, we wound our way across a couple of ridges and into a swamp and then up the other side. We finally ran into some sign and split up a little to sort it out. Dad swung south and I headed north. He came on the radio shortly after and said he had found where the tracks exited the area. Happy to leave the mess behind, I caught up to him and we started in.

Tracking deer together with a partner is a lot of fun and, if you're lucky, the dragging will be only half as hard. I get to share the day with someone, usually my dad, and there is the benefit of a second set of eyes scanning for the buck. Of course, there is also twice as much noise, movement and smell. There are a variety of ways to track together and a lot of how it is done depends on the personalities of the hunters involved. It is important to pick someone that you share similar hunting attributes with. It should also be someone who you'd be as happy to have them shoot the buck as if you had. Usually one guy is the tracker, following the buck and doing the bulk of the ground work, while the other plays the role of stalker, scanning for the deer the whole time, following the tracker up front. Safety is paramount in this situation, so calm heads in the presence of a buck are necessary, especially by the stalker in the rear.

As we moved ahead on the track, it was apparent the buck was with a doe and her fawn, meaning there were extra eyes around. This can be a blessing, as often the buck will hang with the doe and not make a long trek across the country. I've also had it be a curse, where I jump the fawn and it runs ahead, alerting the whole group. These deer fed a couple more times and we diligently sorted it out. Dad would stay on the last sure sign while I moved forward. When I found his track again, Dad would catch up. We weren't gaining a lot of ground this way, but we were keeping things organized and had all day to get caught up to these deer.

Weaving our way through their nighttime ramblings, we finally found where the buck and doe split up, their tryst coming to an end. During the rut, one of two things tends to happen at this point. The buck will either strike off in search of another doe or he will settle down to feed and bed for a while to recover before seeking out a new partner. This buck made his way back into the long swamp we had previously crossed and made a rub. I wrongly suspected we might be in for a long chase. Then he fed and meandered a bit so we slowed down. Creeping through the swamp, I followed the track across a noisy brook in a small opening and stayed with it as it paralleled the stream's bank. Dad came out of the tree line trailing me by about 15 yards. With my eyes down on the track, I heard Dad's rifle go off.

Surprised, I snapped my head up. My first thought was that Dad was shooting at a snowshoe hare or a grouse on the ground. These are things he has been known to do when his focus wanes. In the brief second it took to start to swing around to look back at Dad, I caught the buck in the act of standing up from his bed.

Wasting no time, I pulled up and shot. The buck bolted out of sight. I finished my turn toward Dad with a look of shock on my face that was mirrored in his. Taking a few minutes to catch our breath, we conversed excitedly. Dad related that as he stepped past the tree he had seen the buck turn its head while watching me. Laying no more than 35 yards away, I had been completely unaware.

Dad and I with The Grazer Buck. Vermont 2007. 5 points and 148 pounds.

Keeping my eyes down on a track is a mistake that has often cost me. The tendency I have is to want to see each foot step that buck takes. Afraid I'll miss some important piece of evidence on the ground, I've been known to miss seeing a buck nearby. Learning to just glance at the track, rather than stare at it, has led to more bucks in my crosshairs.

Making our way to where the buck had been bedded, we found good sign of a hit. Taking up the track after discussing our options, we hunted along slowly, following a good blood trail the whole way. Within 60 yards we found the buck piled up. We thanked him for his life, dressed him out and began to drag him toward an old tote road we knew was nearby. Wanting to see where we had hit the buck, we looked him over. Finding only one hole and knowing we had each shot left some questions unanswered. Chatting happily, we began the drag. Under and over blowdowns, uphill out of the swamp, it wasn't easy. Getting to a log landing, I left Dad to finish the downhill portion while I scooted along to get the truck.

Upon my return, Dad had some news. With the drag finished, he had inspected the buck and found a raking wound across the top of his back. The angle strongly suggested it was Dad who had caused it. It mattered little, as this was a double-team buck we were both proud of. It did, however, earn him the nickname "Grazer" at camp for the next year, until he shot another buck that we double teamed, dropping that one its tracks.

The Twenty Minute Buck

The second weekend of the Vermont 2008 rifle season started with falling snow. This got me fired up to find a buck track to follow. Dad and I left camp to try to find one to double team on. Unfortunately the deer were holed up and not moving in the snow. We met back at camp around noon to have some lunch and strategize for the afternoon. After some discussion, we decided to drive about twenty minutes to a friend's camp a few miles away and hunt the stretch of woods there for a change of scenery.

After pulling into their driveway, we got our gear together quickly. The weather remained blustery, so the deer still probably hadn't been

Dad with the Twenty Minute Buck he shot in 2008 on another double team tracking adventure we shared. Vermont 5 points 165 pounds.

moving much. There was a bit of an open field to the east with some rolling terrain that had been cut a few years before out beyond it to the north. We skirted into the woods, intending to stay on the western edge of the field and head for the cut terrain. Within minutes of ducking into the soft wood, we stumbled into a pile of fresh deer tracks. The deer had tucked themselves in the thick cover to stay out of the weather. We began to sort out the tracks to see if there was something to follow when we jumped the deer downhill from us. Neither Dad nor I had seen enough to know what they were or even how many, but we had freshened everything up in a hurry. Rather than sorting out the mess, we slipped over to the beds. There was a medium sized buck among the group of three we now knew we had stirred up!

Slipping along in the blustery weather, the running tracks led us downhill in the thick cover. As we approached the edge of the select cut area, I followed the tracks out into the open. Dad was behind me and as he reached the edge of the thicker cover he looked to his left. He caught movement. Pulling up his rifle, he saw a buck poking his head out from behind a large spruce. Wasting no time he put the crosshairs on the buck's neck, his only shot option, and fired. The buck immediately disappeared from view.

There was no doubt about what he was shooting at this time. I scanned quickly, hoping for my chance, but saw nothing. I looked back to Dad who quickly pointed to where he had seen the buck. I hustled over and found him at the base of that large spruce. A quick finishing shot put the buck down for good. It seemed that we had hardly gotten started and it was over. I checked the buck's back tracks. He had circled to stay in the thick cover and was probably hoping to slip around us. Twenty minutes after we left the truck, we had a buck down.

We dragged the buck for about twenty minutes out to the field and then loaded him in the truck. We were back at camp before dark. 'Grazer' lost his nickname, though it pops up from time to time. The celebrating lasted into the night, albeit for a little longer than twenty minutes.

Chapter 5

BARE GROUND

Sunshine Buck

I cut my teeth on big woods hunting in northern NH, yet shooting a buck there eluded me for a long time. I've had close calls, misses and bucks shot in front of me. I learned many tracking lessons there. In 2016, I felt the need to really try to close the deal on a NH buck. The way my hunting partners and I break down our trips, early November is typically devoted to NH. This is due to its relatively close proximity to my home in northern VT and the early muzzleloader season, which often includes a 'doe day' for antlerless harvest for those hunters who want to put meat in the freezer early. This varies with management goals and population fluctuations, but is a pretty regular occurrence.

This particular season found us exploring some new areas. I got into some good buck sign near fresh cuts, so I was excited. We were driving about 90 minutes each way daily and, while there had been snow, it had melted pretty quickly leaving us a lot of bare ground hunting. My father, Uncle Ron and I pounded around pretty hard, covering territory and still hunting areas with buck sign. Both my uncle and Dad missed deer early in the muzzleloader season. With the VT season fast approaching, my uncle shot a doe on the first day of rifle season and wrapped up his season in NH.

With Dad at work and Ron tagged out, I headed back again. There was a skiff of snow and I decided to head back to an old haunt. The snow petered out by midday but I had found sign of a good buck in the area. The next day I headed back to that spot, but found some other trucks parked in the area. Respecting their first arrival and keeping good woods etiquette, I kept going and decided to hit the large mountain from a different direction, suspecting those guys wouldn't head up into the steep terrain. Getting parked, I started hiking in, slabbing the terrain in the crunchy leaves, waiting for the sun to give me those magical, early, bare ground hours of good sneaking in melted frost soft stepping.

Fresh scrapes and rubs found during bare ground hunting can indicate there is good buck activity.

I gained some elevation and climbed the last really steep section. Doing this allowed me to get into rugged terrain generally away from the pressure of most other hunters. The direction I went was different from how most people would chose to hunt there. Rather than walking in on an old log road or snowmobile trail, I often head in perpendicular to those easier walking trails depending on the wind. I try to do things that other people won't as a way to get around a buck's usual defenses. Thinking about the stage of the rut also made this tactic worthwhile, being on the early side of things. It is also likely that the bucks had no desire to actively breed during the day because the temperatures had been quite warm. Add in the fact that the season was almost two weeks old and it is easy to imagine that, due to the hunting pressure, they had secured themselves far up and away from the activity of people. Later in the rut bucks might have been with does at this time of day, not necessarily bedded alone up high.

I caught my breath and cruised along a deer trail into some fresher sign. I jumped a deer. I hit my deer call and waited. I could hear it walking on the other side of some trees, just catching a flicker of movement here and there. I moved a little, grunting now and then to keep the deer interested. Raising my rifle as the deer crossed a gap, I saw a piece of antler around an ear, but no more. The deer took any decision to shoot out of my hands as he took off, escaping to the south. I snuck up to where the buck had been and saw that the young fella had made some good choices for a bedding area. He had good cover, an escape route, food nearby and the wind in his favor from most routes (but not the direction I had come from). After a short break, I decided to carry on along the mountain.

Moving into the wind, I cruised down one short hill and then started up another along the ridge line. Considering the wind is important. It doesn't have to be in my face all the time, but at least quartering into it is helpful. While it will swirl around in the mountains in any number of directions, trying to keep from being directly upwind of a deer can increase the odds of an encounter. The wind wasn't perfect to hunt this area when I started the day, but I worked my way around for the wind to be better based on where I wanted to go, and then navigated the rougher country to get into that area. It can be helpful to think like a buck. I try to picture where he expects to encounter danger and how he would use that expectation to select a bedding location. Once there is an idea of where a buck might be bedded, I select a route to effectively get in to that area while avoiding doing what that buck expects.

As I snuck along, I saw a pond below me with the sun striking the eastern facing slope ahead. Marking the area on my GPS, I proceeded along and caught sight of something that looked out of place in the sunshine. The moment I paused, that buck was on his feet and gone. In the glimpse I got of him in that one bound, I saw enough of his antlers to get my heart racing. Hoping to stop him, I grunted and bleated on my call then waited. While he had disappeared into a thick screen of cover, there were some open areas to the west and south and I hoped he might circle to get my wind. After 30 minutes, I headed over to his bed and followed his running and then walking tracks as far as I could. I saw where he had stopped to watch his back track, but he never tried to circle. The ground dried quickly and I lost his track, so I still hunted along likely deer trails but didn't see him again.

Water bodies are important terrain features to notice in addition to the general topography. That pond that the buck bedded above likely created a funnel for movement. The steep terrain that helped create that pond also made the buck feel more secure. Often when you are hunting bare ground, brook valleys into higher damp country will lead you to buck sign. A buck's signpost rubs are often found in these locations. Also, with modern logging practices, these areas tend to be left alone to protect riparian habitat. This protection creates edge cover that whitetails prefer.

Like many bare ground bucks, one encounter was all I got. It seems to take a lot of effort to even see a deer in these conditions and shooting one is even more challenging. Considering deer densities and the size of the big woods, for me, stalking and still hunting are vastly more enjoyable and more likely to be successful than sitting in a stand. Both offer an opportunity to explore new country. While sometimes frustrating, I find that locating sign when the ground is bare leads to more success when the snow hits. Time in the woods chasing bucks is never wasted.

A signpost rub that was recently freshened. Connecting pieces of buck sign like this can pay off on bare ground or later when it snows.

Trail cameras deployed in-season can give you an idea of who is making the sign you are finding.

Gravel Drag Buck

After going to our VT camp for the traditional opening weekend festivities, I started heading back to NH. I like the reduced pressure and bigger woods. With Friday off, I made my 12th 90-minute drive, focusing on a new area I discovered just the day before. I had found a freshly logged stretch of woods, a gated road and a scrape line. I decided to tackle this area from a slightly different direction, taking the wind and the terrain into consideration as I headed in. Still without snow, I was becoming accustomed to the slower, sneakier pace of still hunting. This morning things were damp, always an advantage.

Truck parked, I headed across a brook into some lower, swampier terrain, planning to head uphill on the other side after crossing the gated road. I cruised the edges of two older cuts along the way, seeing deer tracks and feeding sign. Ducking into the beauty strip of timber between those cuts, I got onto a nice deer trail. I could see fresh tracks here and there.

Learning to slow down in good sign has led to more sightings for me. I used to cover ground very quickly, always aiming to get somewhere, and would end up seeing a lot of flags bouncing off through the trees. While I still jump a lot of deer, poking through likely areas a bit more slowly has helped. The challenge is being able to get a shot in these situations. When there is snow I have a higher confidence level about what is going on ahead of me and I can slow down a bit more and stay focused. On bare ground, this concentration is harder to maintain. When in good sign and likely areas, I find it is important to hunt like I know the buck is right there.

Poking along, I noticed a downed softwood tree with a lot of old man's beard. It had been browsed pretty heavily. Thinking the tracks looked pretty fresh and the cover good, the thought crossed my mind that this would be a good spot to encounter a deer. Remembering the scrape line I had discovered from the day before, it certainly could be a buck.

Continuing to sneak along, I was only about 30 yards away from the feeding sign when a deer jumped up, making a couple bounds. I bleated quickly with my mouth as I pulled up my rifle. Scope at 2x, I could see parts of a deer standing 50 yards away. Heart pounding, I turned the scope magnification up and pulled the rifle to my shoulder again. Now I had a bigger picture of the deer but it was still unidentified. I then slid a step to my left and I could see an antler. Now I needed to find a clear shot. Sliding back to the right a little, I squatted down to get the crosshairs below a branch and fired a round. The buck disappeared from sight. Working the action as I quickly moved forward, I saw him get his front feet under him, head up. At 35 yards, I put another round behind his shoulder and he went down. Running up to him, I put a final round in his neck to end it quickly.

An example of the thick boreal forest these bucks can inhabit.

With the mix of sadness, accomplishment and thankfulness that typically accompanies the killing of an animal, I set to the task of dressing him out. I've learned to take my time with this task and reflect on the moment. I replayed the many days and miles that led to it.

One constant battle I have had in my growth as a big woods hunter is to recognize and see deer quickly. The deer can be almost anywhere at any time. If he is still and you are on the move it becomes harder to pick him out. I have found that the more often I see and encounter deer, the more likely I am to develop a sight picture of what I am looking for. This includes bedded deer and pieces of deer anatomy that look out of place. In the fall when there isn't snow, the small white patches on a deer can stand out more than an antler or their body. The key is to be able to rapidly identify that deer so there is time to react. With the sunshine buck earlier in the season, if I'd identified him lying there a step earlier,

The Gravel Drag Buck. New Hampshire 2016 8 points and 155 pounds.

I might have had a chance to do something more to result in getting a shot. While I often call after jumping a deer, my results vary. I think that once a buck feels threatened by the presence of a predator inside his comfort zone, it becomes much harder to stop him and make something happen.

I was broken out of my reverie by a human voice. I realized I wasn't all that far from the gated road. A guide and his sport were apparently walking up it and had heard me shoot, so they yelled "Did you get him?"

I replied with an emphatic "Yes!"

Here again, most people walk the road in. Hunting through the woods made a difference. The guide came down and helped me drag the buck out to that road. We all chatted for a moment, then I thanked them as they headed off to continue their hunt. I was about a half mile from the gate.

Beginning the drag, I thought going down the road would make it easy. No blowdowns to haul him over, no sticks or stumps to contend with. I learned pretty quickly that having no leaves to drag through made things much more challenging than I anticipated. The relatively even grade of the road offered me little assistance on the downhills and a challenge going uphill as well. The twelve days of hunting leading up to getting my tag in this bucks ear had left my legs tired, getting the half mile to the gate via the road was not going to be the piece of cake I had hoped for. Remembering a story told by my friend Marc, who uses his horse to drag moose out of the woods, I found my way to the side of the road to get the buck in the leaves and the drag got a little more reasonable. Thankfully the buck was not a monster; ninety minutes later I had him and my gear stashed near the gate. Running the mile and a half up the road to my truck was easy as I felt as light as a feather. I drove back and got my bare ground NH buck loaded up, out to the tagging station and finally home to VT.

Chapter 6

CATCHING UP

First Shot

A FTER hunting the big woods of NH for a few years, Dad and I decided to make a leap into bigger territory by adding in a trip to
northern Maine. The planning started the winter before, booking a cabin
and doing a lot of map research. After settling on a couple logging road
systems to get into some good territory, we decided to make a spring
scouting trip. This trip was mostly for us to get a feel for the country
we wanted to hunt. We pulled in late on a Friday and were staying at
the same place we booked for our hunting season. The owner gave us
a couple spots to check out, which was a helpful start. We took a long
drive on Saturday with a couple forays into the woods around some cuts.
Seeing a deer in this country felt like a good omen. We were pumped to
be back for muzzleloader hunting.

An unsuccessful five days of hunting during Thanksgiving week in NH
were behind us. We headed home to VT to do some laundry, get a good
night's rest and then repack, grab our muzzleloaders and head to Maine.
We were hunting the week of the northern tier muzzleloader season. After arriving at our cabin Sunday afternoon, we settled in, anxious for the
next day. Snow had arrived in the region the Friday before we got there
and there hadn't been anything fresh since, so we'd be hunting on old
snow. While less than ideal, it was still vastly better than no snow.

Monday and Tuesday of that week found us checking a few of the spots
we scouted on that older snow. One area was a dud without much in the

way of sign. The next area was 29 miles in on a logging road and there was only one set of old tire tracks in there. Wondering if everyone else knew something we didn't, we headed in anyway. Hunting up and around the mountain, I was able to find what looked like two different good bucks. The tracks were a couple days old, but it was nice to see there were some bucks around. Not hunting them specifically, I followed the tracks hoping to cut something fresher, but that didn't happen. Wednesday the snow was disappearing and we didn't see much again. Doubt was creeping in, but at least there was snow in the forecast.

Fresh snow on Thursday really brightened things up for us. The snow came late in the night, making it tough to strike a track from the road. We parked and headed into the woods, deciding to split up to hunt for a buck to track. We planned to meet in the woods if it worked out, otherwise we'd simply rendezvous back at the truck at the end of the day. In a whole different area from where we had been hunting, I managed to cut a track in the woods at 10:30 in some steep country. Following his wandering, I knew the track wasn't more than a couple hours old. I jumped him up around noon, not recognizing from the sign he was leaving that he would be bedded down. I gave him what Dad and I refer to as 'Hal's half-hour', after advice we'd heard from well-known deer tracker Hal Blood, who's cabin we were renting. Taking up the track with a buck just in front of me, I expected a long chase because that's what I was used to from tracking heavily pressured VT bucks. Instead, this buck took me out of the steep country down into a softwood swamp and then toward a cut. As I was sneaking along, I noticed a deer up ahead. Creeping a bit closer but not wanting to spook him, I could see it was the buck I was tracking. He was feeding in the green growth on a tote road, scratching it up with his hooves and taking some nips, then tossing his head back. This was the first time I ever had a buck forget all about me and return to normal behavior after being spooked. It was only 1 p.m., just an hour since I'd jumped him! I was getting nervous so I crept as close as I dared, about 75 yards away. I lined him up in my peep sights and took a shot at the broadside feeding buck. He immediately ran off. I reloaded and made my way to where he had been feeding. No sign of a hit. I tracked him headed away from the truck until 3 p.m. then turned and headed for the truck. Mildly dejected, I was also excited to have caught up to big woods Maine buck.

It used to feel like I would never catch up to a buck I was tracking. While this does happen, there are so many factors involved that I don't worry about it anymore. I really don't know what the last day or week has looked like for that animal. He might have been on a long trek and needed to recover. He may have been chased by a hunter the day before and was just trying to get into remote country to stay safe. He might be rested up and ready to look for another doe to breed. The time of year and the buck's individual personality will also dictate the day's outcome. When I combine that with my own particular circumstances – how tired I am, the snow conditions, the terrain; there is a wide swath of possibilities. The bottom line is that I now expect to catch up to every buck I track. With that expectation, it is easier to make smart decisions about how to play the end game. This also helps to keep me alert to sign that indicates he is somewhere close, instead of plowing along mindlessly. In this case, I could have snuck a little closer to that first Maine buck I caught up to, but I was so amazed to catch up to him that I simply rushed things in my excitement.

Melting Snow Buck

Snow is a key ingredient for deer trackers. We obsess over it and become amateur weathermen, trying to predict when and where it will fall. We are also quite picky about it. We want it at the right temperature and consistency, to fall at the right time and in just the right amount. We don't want all of this for just one day either, but for a week or two or three. Unfortunately, all this obsessing doesn't do much for us. The snow will be what it is on that day and we need to make the best of it.

Dad and I again found ourselves in Maine for our traditional Thanksgiving week hunt. A storm that came late the night before the first day left us struggling to find tracks, because the deer had holed up until the weather turned. Getting very little going day one, on day two we split up in an area we used to hunt to see what was going on. Discovering very little and with warmer temperatures in the forecast, it looked like we needed to get it done on the third day.

We headed to a new area I had briefly scouted the previous spring. The road was rough, limiting access in one respect. But it wasn't far from a main road, so a lot of guys drove by thinking they had to get deeper in the woods to find a buck track. The mountain had snow but it looked like today would be the last of it. We split up with plans to rally at the top of the mountain. I swung north and east while dad headed more to the west, also moving north. I crossed an older buck track that piqued my interest due to its size, but the age of it kept me from jumping on it- I wanted something smoking fresh.

As I gained elevation, there wasn't much for sign. At our brief meet-up Dad said that he hadn't seen much either. Disappointed, we formulated a new plan and headed down the mountain. I was going to take that older set of tracks we had both crossed down lower. Dad set over, further to the west to swing outside what we had already covered.

Dropping down toward the older track, I noticed it was turning into a nice day. The snow was melting pretty quickly and the reduced amount down low would vanish even faster. When I cut the track I moved along pretty quickly, knowing I had already lost time. The buck's tracks headed generally west and I cruised past where Dad had the cut track. The buck stayed on the low side of the cut; he looked like he was on a mission. A buck on a mission headed downhill can be tough to catch. He is often in search of a doe and will check on those within his range. This could mean a trek of 10 miles for the buck, as well as the hunter following. Given the fact this was an older track already, my hopes of catching him were fading. At this time of day and with the snow departing, this was my last chance.

I should have considered the time of year and the phase of the rut. There is much discussion surrounding the timing of the rut and how it applies to deer hunters. Mating season can vary based on the region. For a deer tracker specifically, this knowledge can help make good decisions while tracking. The buck I'd followed was in post-rut, but I hadn't thought of that.

The buck worked across the bottom of the cut and was slabbing across and slightly down the mountain, moving slowly toward the road we had driven in on but significantly further west than where we parked. Exiting the cut, he made a scrape and his tracks began to wander a bit. A fresher buck track of the same size crossed the older track. Suspecting it was the same buck, I stayed on the old track a little longer and found his empty bed with tracks walking away. Mildly surprised that he had bedded and, by the location, I kept the pace up. At this point, Dad arrived on the scene, taking a more direct route down. We decided to stay together and double team the buck, knowing we'd have to work pretty hard to catch the rested buck on the melting snow.

The buck crossed the road we had driven in on beyond where we parked and was meandering through some thicker terrain. The snow cover was much thinner down low, so the tracking was getting difficult. This required a couple different techniques to stay on the track as he began crossing more open areas. Often an obvious deer trail was visible, so we'd stay on that until we hit snow on the other side and could confirm we were still on his track. If we didn't see his track, Dad would go back to the last known spot and I'd circle from snow patch to snow patch looking, much like we were on a blood trail. A couple of rounds of this, through some small cuts and across another old road, had us almost done for the day. Then the track entered some darker timber.

With slightly better snow, we decided to keep the pace up. Seeing where the buck fed, I kept moving right along on the track. Suddenly, a deer stood up from behind a blowdown 70 yards away. In the instant it took for me to pull my eyes up from the ground to look at the buck, he was gone. Dad, trailing behind me, had seen him stand, but had only started to pull up his rifle; it never got to his shoulder. We stayed on the buck as long as we could after that but, as the snow dripped away, it became clear one chance was all we were going to get. That buck melted into our memories.

When discussion among hunters turns to the whitetail rut, I think we run into a bunch of problems. The first is defining what we mean by "the rut." As an umbrella term, the rut is defined as the whitetail breeding season. There needs to be an anchor point in this discussion and I think it has to do with actual conception of a fawn by a buck breeding a doe. From there, descriptions can move outward toward the behavior most seen by bucks around this act. There is not much evidence of lunar phases predicting the rut very accurately, so the closest estimate is to back date the arrival of fawns on the ground in the spring by the deer's 200 day gestation period. As fawns begin to arrive in the late spring and early summer, we can expect that their mothers hid them for a week or two. By these estimates, most dates of conception in northern New England are between November 13th and November 20th.

I take a buck-centric point of view of the whitetail breeding season, because I am concerned with how that impacts my hunting decisions. The phases of the rut describe the actions of the bucks and what is likely to happen while tracking. It is important to note that actual breeding is ultimately driven by the female members of the herd, though the behaviors we hunters normally associate with the rut are associated with bucks. A buck will breed any time a doe is ready. Hormonal changes and the presence of ready-to-breed does result in what hunters see in the woods. The phases also blend together and overlap considerably, with individual bucks drifting in and out of them as fall progresses toward winter. Each buck also has his own personality based on previous experiences, his rank in the herd and his mood on a particular day.

Early fall is really before the rut, when bucks are feeding and their hormone levels are just starting to rise. This phase would encompass the time from when they rub the velvet off their antlers until they start to actively compete with other bucks. This time of year is when a buck is most predictable, focused primarily on feeding within the core of his range, with light scraping and rubbing activity close to home. In the North

Country, I think of this period covering late September until about the 20th of October. Many areas do not have a rifle season open and there is often not snow for tracking, but this is a good time to scout and find early primary scrapes and check on signpost rubs. Buck weights will be much higher this time of year.

Pre-rut is when bucks start to expand their range and get fired up about breeding. They will begin to cover more territory and aggressively scrape and rub. Encounters with other bucks of equal size tend to be violent. Young bucks are often already checking does, while older bucks know the drill and are just keeping tabs on everything. These older bucks will often still be feeding heavily to prepare for the rut. If there is an early season snow, it pays to know the home range of these bucks to find a track and then hunt him as if he is close. Without snow, sticking around active scrape lines and still hunting between signpost rubs is a good idea.

Seeking begins around November 7th up north, when bucks begin to look for those first does that will stand for breeding. But they are very unlikely to find one. Scrapes and rubs will be hit opportunistically as a buck travels through his range but, overall, bucks are now much harder to pattern. They will also spend more time on their feet during daylight hours if the weather is cool enough, scent checking doe groups throughout the range. This is usually done from higher ground. If it is warm, most of this phase, along with the subsequent breeding phases, will occur at night. Tracking a wandering buck now can lead to a long track job, though he can be caught when he is frustrated and making rubs and scrapes. These activities slow him down and he'll be distracted.

Chasing behavior begins to happen just prior to the 15th. Bucks chase through the breeding phase as well, when they can sense a doe is entering her estrous period. This occurs because the doe will be ready to breed soon, but she won't stand yet. It is not unusual in areas with good numbers of bucks to see multiple bucks trailing a single doe. Bucks that have found and bred a doe will seek and then chase another if she is almost ready, continuing this cyclic behavior throughout the nearly two week active breeding cycle. Depending on where in the chase a buck is, it may

Buck working a community scrape during the pre-rut.

or may not be possible to catch him. On the plus side, there is a chance to encounter other bucks along the trail of this doe. This is usually when the classic but somewhat rare story of people back-tracking a doe and running into a buck happens.

Breeding likely begins to happen around the 13th of November and can continue for 7-14 days, depending on the local herd structure and buck-to-doe ratio. Does will stand to be bred and can create a 'lock down' effect where it is harder to find a buck wandering. Bucks that are with a doe in this time period will be hesitant to leave her, making for interesting tracking as there are more eyes and ears to contend with. But, thankfully, the buck is not focused solely on his survival. Once the doe has been bred, a buck will often search for another, though he will usually feed briefly and bed for several hours between does. These are the bucks that are found alone on a mountain at daylight who will head out on a long chase if jumped.

Post-rut bucks will still check on does, but they do not range as far and wide as they were just a week earlier. Much like the pre-rut, there is a lot more feeding and resting, this time for recovery. Usually around the beginning of December, snow and temperature conditions may dictate deer movement toward a yard, though a few may stay in their fall home range. A buck tracked after the rut will often be alone and easier to catch. Weights of bucks this time of year will be down, but his rack will still look nice.

General knowledge of what is going on with the rut is one piece of information for selecting where and how to locate a buck and hunt him. Then it is important to react to the specific situation you are presented with in terms of snow, weather and hunting pressure. With the Melting Snow Buck, if I'd thought a little more about the fact that this was a late season buck, I might not have continued to crank along the track after we had freshened it up and saw the feeding sign. Late season bucks don't usually travel too far. Their priorities are mostly rest and recovery, with short forays to look for breeding opportunities. You have to read the sign accurately and make the best decision you can based on that information.

Thanksgiving Sandwich Buck

In 2011, Dad and I headed to Jackman for the 4th week of the Maine season. We were staying at an outfitter's cabin with a meal plan, but hunting on our own. There was good food and a small group of good guys. There were five hunters and one guide, plus the staff at the table for each meal. One gentleman was being guided while the other father/son pair was hunting on their own as well.

With no snow on the ground, Dad and I decided to split up and scout some unfamiliar territory on the road system we had success on during muzzleloader season the last year. We spent Monday and Tuesday covering ground both in the woods and on the road. We split up morning and afternoon, essentially scouting/still hunting two areas per day. Dad managed to see one unidentified deer doing this and I saw two moose.

Tuesday night into Wednesday a storm moved in and by the time it was done we had about 6-8 inches. We took two trucks in on Wed and hunted different ends of the area where we had each missed a buck last year. Knowing the deer would be hunkered down, I moved quickly looking for tracks, hoping to jump a buck up and chase him around. Finally around 11, I cut a track and it was relatively small, but I followed it hoping it would lead me onto something bigger. I never caught up to it and never ran onto another track. Dad saw one doe and nothing else.

Thursday morning we went out with high hopes of finding a buck track to double team. We did a good loop in the truck and the best track, definitely a 200 pounder, already had a guy on it so we went back to our second choice. A buck and doe together worked into a gaggle of deer – typical barnyard-of-tracks situation. It took a while to sort out, including lots of up and down a pretty severe hill (or cliff, as Dad called it). By 9:30 we had put on a few miles and Dad was getting whipped because he had overdone it on Wednesday in the storm. When we crossed a road headed away from the truck at 12:30, Dad decided to hunt his way back, saying he would pick me up near where we split up. I stayed on the buck for a few more hours and didn't catch up to him – he was well rested. I did track him into another group of deer that had a buck with them. That buck rubbed a tree and dragged his feet around very aggressively. I couldn't tell that they fought, but there were a lot of running tracks. I turned and headed for the road shortly after this as it was late in the day. Good day tracking, but no deer sightings. Thanksgiving dinner back at the main cabin was tasty. The outfitter made the leftovers into a delicious sandwich of turkey, dressing and cranberry sauce for the next day.

Friday morning started out the same as Thursday, looking for tracks. Temps had warmed, so it was like a fresh start. We were headed into a different stretch, closer to where we had seen the big boy's track the day before. As we got close to a turn in the road we wanted to check out, we saw where the guide and hunter staying at camp had parked their truck. Now thinking we'd go somewhere different, we did a quick map look-over and headed left instead of right. At this point it was getting late and, as always, I was antsy to get in the woods. We decided to park and split up, heading into the woods to look for tracks.

I walked back up the road we had driven in on and cut what I thought was a brand new, ultra-fresh track. After getting in touch with Dad, I headed in after the buck, thinking I was going to be right on top of him. After 30 min I realized I read it wrong and we had missed that track on the drive in. Nonetheless I decided to stay on it, but now with a little faster pace. He was obviously cruising for does as there was a steady pace and no real wandering. Making up time, we saw where he had come up on his own back track, he then did some feeding and bedded briefly. He walked out of the bed, which is always a good sign. Things got much fresher at this point. He proceeded to check doe groups pretty quickly; you could tell he wasn't finding what he wanted. He'd mix up with them, they'd all line out together and fairly soon his track would veer off all alone, on to the next group. He crossed a road and a beaver dam, made a rub and found some more does as he stayed on the move. Crossing another road, his tracks were on top of everything else. We gained time with each group he checked.

By now Dad and I had settled into a pretty good rhythm. Dad's legs were fresh compared to the rough day he had Thursday. With our third day on snow, I had worn off a little of my typical high-speed excitement. Generally as we go, I keep tabs on the track and Dad scans the woods. Depending on terrain and pace he may drift a little or hang back. With a few years of practice behind us, I just keep doing my thing, trying to spot the buck before he does, which doesn't usually happen.

The buck moved into another group of 3-4 deer and we were sneaking along through the hardwood whips, headed uphill. Dad swung off to the left up onto a ridge where he could see a little better as I stayed with the herd. Continuing to poke along I spotted a doe off to my left at about 100-125 yards, not where the deer I was on were headed. Shortly after I spotted her, she caught me moving. With the wind in my face I was

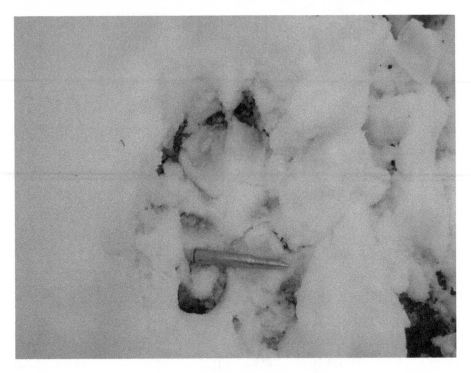

Thanksgiving Sandwich buck track.

downwind of her. She turned tail and started blowing with every bound she made up the valley. I figured that was going to spook everything within miles. I moved though the softwood ahead of me to see if the buck I was tracking had bedded there. He hadn't. The whole group had kept moving. Getting to the other side, I found a good spot to sit and wait for Dad and hopefully let things calm down. I pulled out my delicious sandwich as it was now after 11.

Dad came along behind me and, as he crested the knob out of the softwood, he saw me. Within a few seconds, he saw a deer ahead of me, about 100-150 yards from him. He put the scope on it and thought he saw horns, but said when he didn't see me reacting at all he thought it must be a doe that I was watching. I hadn't actually seen the deer at this point, but did in short order- I could see his hooves in some thick growth at about 30 paces as he was back tracking. I think he was checking on

Thanksgiving Sandwich Buck. Maine 2011 10 points and 182 pounds.

the blowing doe he likely heard when I spooked her. I readied myself and slowly put down my sandwich. When he came into view with his head down, bird dogging along, I pulled up my 760 carbine. He saw me move and when he picked his head up I fully saw his rack and body. I knew instantly that he was a buck I wanted to shoot. I put the bead at the base of his neck and then slid it slightly down to the point of his near shoulder and pulled the trigger before he could take off. He hunched up and rocked onto his back legs, then tipped over. I readied another bullet in case he got up, but he was still. The emotion drained from me and I put my head in my hands. All the hard work and effort had culminated in this one moment. Dad came up to me and clapped me on the back and we hugged and celebrated.

We dressed the deer, took pictures, checked tracks and began the drag. Dad helped for a bit, and then he headed for the truck as I finished getting the deer to the road. What a wonderful feeling it was as we loaded him into the truck and headed out to register him and hang him at camp and tell the story to each other over a beer. All our hunting trips are fun and special, but taking this buck with my Dad like we did was about as good as it gets – until the next one we shoot together!

Chapter 7

STILL LEARNING

Running Buck

ADVENTURE is a big part of hunting for me. When big woods deer hunting, all I realistically look for is one chance per week. Often, the satisfaction in tracking a buck is in making the right calls to catch him, even if you don't get to drag him out. While that doesn't put meat in the freezer, getting close lets you know you're improving. You gain experience with each of these encounters. The line between success and failure is a thin one and even if you do everything right, the outcome may not be what you want. Conversely, there are a lot of times you can do things wrong and still put a tag in a buck's ear. The important part of becoming a better tracker is to focus on the process, not just the results.

Thursday morning of another fourth week of rifle season in Maine, Dad and I woke to 10 inches of fresh snow on the ground, making for two excited hunters. Thirteen miles into our journey, my truck started acting funny so we headed back to camp to trade it out for my father's less beat up truck. With that, we lost the advantage of being on the road early for tracks. By the time we got back out there, there were a lot of people around. We drove around and checked out some brand new areas but never really got things started, much to my disappointment.

Friday was a better day. We managed to pick up a medium-sized buck track in the woods and, while sorting out his nightly wanderings, found a better one. We took the track and followed the buck as he headed up into some bluffs on the Canadian border. Sneaking up through the rugged terrain, I knew we would only have one crack at him. By 1 p.m. I came across his empty bed within sight of the border. He had the drop on us from a long way off and we finally ended up pushing him into Canada without a sighting.

Now down to Saturday, we had to make something happen. Daylight found us staring at a medium-sized track on the road next to a rather large beaver bog. With time winding down, we got the truck parked out of the way and headed in. Sorting through the frozen tracks, we were able to follow the buck, a doe and her fawn for a while. As they led us around the bog, the track of a bigger-bodied buck crossed their paths and we split off on his track around 9 a.m.

We tracked him in a long, straight line headed east as he checked a couple of doe groups and we found an older, frozen bed that he had left. With the day warming up, we kept the pace up until noon-time when his sign started to appear really fresh in the sun-warmed snow. We were only an hour or two behind him at the most. The sign indicated he had fed again and I thought we were going to catch him in a bed, so we went into sneak mode in likely looking areas. This was steep country with lots of places for him to lie down. His tracks continued to meander around, on and off old logging roads and through old blown down trees. After a while of this, he made a fresh scrape and kept walking.

At that point, it didn't really seem that he was going to bed so we decided to pick up the pace on him again. Approaching 2 p.m. with more than 6 miles back to the truck, something needed to happen soon.

The buck made a big circle and crossed our tracks at that same scrape about an hour after we had first been there. Another 20 minutes along the track and I saw where he stood and moved around, then his bounding tracks; we had caught up to him and spooked him while he was on his feet. Having hunted this general area in the past, I knew there was a good sized clear cut ahead. The track headed in that direction. I got a move on and, when I saw the track headed into the edge of the cut, I started running up the hills and trotting down them. Three ridgelines in, maybe a half mile of that speedy pace, I finally spotted the buck. He was about 150 yards away on the move, out of a small valley and headed over the next ridge. I tried to steady myself to make a good shot with my peep-sighted .30-06 and got off two before he disappeared out of sight.

I reloaded and headed along the buck's track to confirm this was the same deer we'd been tracking. As Dad caught back up to me, we scoured the area looking for sign of a hit. With no evidence that I had connected, we stayed on him through the rest of the cut. He had run the length of it and exited near a log landing. Knowing he was unhurt, it was time for us to turn and head for the truck. We cut across to a road and had a nice walk back as the sun set on that season, sharing the mixed emotions of success and failure. We had made decisions leading to a big buck encounter that we might not have otherwise had, yet the tough shot might have been easier if I'd been just a little stealthier in my approach. You never really know until you've tried and missed. All things considered, I'll likely do a lot of the same things if faced with a similar situation in the future. There is never a perfect decision while on the track...

Old Tracks Buck

Dad and I switched up our area in Maine in 2016 based on some hunting and scouting we had done over the previous 18 months. We had some great bucks on trail camera that had us pretty excited. The forecast was good so hopes were high. We arrived in a new camp for our traditional Thanksgiving week rifle hunt. The first couple days we had snow but were challenged to find a good buck to track. Finally getting one going, we followed him around and then through a nasty swamp. After hitting a signpost rub, he linked up with a group of does that we ended up busting as we exited some thick cedars. He made a couple of scrapes and then headed off to parts unknown to close out the day.

Two days later, with fresh snow on the ground, I decided to make a big loop up and around a high ridgeline. Near noontime, I came around the backside of the mountain and cut the track of a very large buck crossing

Freshly hit signpost rub in Maine. Note the bark on top of the snow.

an old logging road. Excited, I headed in on the track as it slabbed across the hill. On the soft snow I snuck along, fully expecting to be right on top of him. As I eased through the cover, I saw a barnyard of tracks where a smaller doe track joined his impressively large set. I began to circle the tracks, which is usually the fastest way to sort these things out, especially when the buck track is that much larger than all the others. As I circled, I'd see the pair of deer exit the area and, as I followed, I'd see where they headed in again. Repeating this several times and cursing the minutes I was wasting, I decided to do a much larger loop to see if I could get this sorted out more efficiently. Back out on the abandoned logging road, I made a big swing down and around the patch of woods, discovering another road on the other side where they'd recently pulled timber off another ridge.

Seeing where this buck had chased the doe out onto that road and then back in, it seemed like these deer might have headed up and over the steep face to the north. I switched directions and swung around without crossing any sign. Taking a deep breath to avoid doing anything rash, I pulled out my GPS and realized I had left one corner of this small section of woods untouched. This spot, protected by the steep section above, was difficult to access, which is probably why these deer holed up there. I began my approach from the east, trying to see one of them before they saw me. Based on all the circles I had done, I'm sure they had scented me but were confident in their safety. Easing in, I heard one of the deer take off, then the other. Unseen, they headed back into the melee of tracks. I worked my way to their running tracks and followed the buck, hoping he would make a mistake. Within 300 yards, I jumped him again without seeing him. That was it. I followed him up and over the mountain without sign of him slowing. When we parted ways, his tracks were headed away from the truck. Having spooked him twice, I didn't think the odds were in my favor for making something happen late in the day. With that, my rifle season encounters were done. With three days off the following week, I would be back to muzzleloader hunting.

On the mountain just shy of a week later, there was snow but no good tracks. A logging operation had moved in on the other side of the mountain. This altered deer movement and limited some of where I could go. My buddy Ben was hunting nearby and had a close encounter, but we both knew the bucks there got big by using a large nasty swamp for protection. Ben ended up taking a mucky bath and eventually left that buck alone. The next morning we were a little frustrated by what had turned into crusty conditions. We headed out to cover an area I was familiar with a couple of hours away. Getting in the woods there well after daylight, I hopped on a smaller buck track. Within three hours, I had the spike horn in my sights as he stood in his bed. I passed on him, but I was thankful I could still track a buck down and see him after my frustrating experiences of the week before. Confidence is a key ingredient when tracking deer. I was down to the last day of my Maine hunting season and I struck out with more of it after catching up to that spike buck.

With no track to take from the drive in, my plan was to walk a couple of miles into an area to see if I could find a good buck to track. I headed into the woods at a brisk pace with my smoke pole slung over my shoulder, hunting first for a track. I crossed around the back of a pond two miles in. I then headed up toward a saddle that had looked good on the map. I saw a few tracks of does and fawns migrating toward their winter yard. I made a big loop looking for a buck track that usually heads off in a separate direction from migrating deer. Jumping two deer, I checked out their beds and decided not to follow. I back tracked them for just a short time and found what I was looking for. The buck track was dull and frozen in; it looked like it was from the day before.

I hurried along in an attempt to get things freshened up. I worked my way through the cluster of ridges at the top of this mountain. The buck track veered north and suddenly there was a similar-sized track but a little fresher, as though made in the night instead of the day before. It broke off the trail, going in the opposite direction before swinging west. Could this be the same buck coming back? I stayed with the old track underneath, trying to determine if this newer track was indeed the same deer. As I sorted it out, I couldn't pick up any difference in the appearance of the tracks other than the change in direction. So, I swung around on the fresh version. Suspecting this was the same buck, I had just gained a lot of time on him.

The buck moved through the woods, crossing doe tracks that were steadily headed south as he headed west. He swung through some thick growth and fed a little, then made a rub. Suddenly his track shifted directions again. I stayed hard after him, thinking I still had a lot of time to gain on him. Suddenly, the buck exploded from his bed and was gone. Frustrated that I hadn't heeded the sign but elated I had made up so much time on what had been a day-old track, I gave the buck 30 minutes then again struck out. He was now swinging south, away from the truck and toward the deer yard. Through some open hardwoods I could see quite far, so it was a shock when two moose took off from the backside of a nearby blowdown. I stopped to let my pounding heart slow down and then took up the trail. The pair of moose followed the deer's tracks and then likely spooked the buck. His tracks indicated he was running again.

As the clock ticked down, the moose and deer that seemed to be running together finally separated. The buck shifted gears and slowed down. He began to head toward some thicker cover. As I headed uphill on his track, there were legs moving just at the edge of my vision. I quickly came to my senses and was able to focus on the buck just as he jumped over the edge of a knoll. The muzzleloader at my shoulder remained silent. I followed him down and across the next valley. This buck was another that wouldn't be riding back to Vermont in my truck. Yet the memory of this hunt, what I did right and wrong, when combined with all the other tracks I've taken over the years will hopefully allow me more success down the road. From failure, growth.

It isn't helpful to spend too much mental energy on second guessing oneself while tracking. Simply make a decision and see how it plays out. As Theodore Roosevelt said, "In any moment of decision, the best thing you can do is the right thing, the next best thing is the wrong thing, and

Moose are a welcome and enjoyable sight on a north woods deer hunt, as long as they don't interfere with the tracking!

the worst thing you can do is nothing." A couple lessons were made clear to me on this hunt, in addition to realizing that confidence when tracking is vital. One was to pay attention to transition zones. That buck was spooked by the moose; he may not have realized that I was still there. Knowing that, I should have realized he would stop to check sooner rather than later. This stop to watch a back track, whether it is you or a moose that jumps a buck, often occurs on the edge of cover where hardwood transitions to softwood, where there is a change in topography or where a clear-cut transitions to forest. All provide the deer an advantage for escape. It is often indicated by a break in the direction they are traveling. I should have recognized the sign in the first place where I jumped him out of his bed and been more careful with my approach. I had been in 'catch-up' mode all day and didn't shift gears appropriately to sneak in on that buck. No matter, it was a successful effort to simply get within range of that buck, given how old the track was when I started it. You have got to get into the game to have a chance.

Chapter 8

KEYS TO SUCCESS

E VERY hunting story has elements of success and failure. As deer trackers, we try to tease out every piece of information that will make us more successful when we have a chance to track the 200-pound buck of our dreams. In every tracking adventure, there seem to be key decisions that are pivotal to a buck being taken. I've attempted to boil down the keys to success on my buck hunts, so that in addition to learning from my many failures, hopefully these lessons can be applied to consistently track down bucks in the big woods of the north. Most of this list includes things that cannot be mastered in a book, they must be experienced. Hopefully, awareness of these items helps shorten your learning curve.

Many of these topics have been covered in a number of excellent books on tracking. I would encourage you to look into what the Benoit Family has produced over several decades, along with more recent work by Hal Blood and the Adirondack Trackers. I have been a student of these trackers since I was young and they offer many good tips and tricks. I'll add my two cents worth here. I would be remiss in not helping other trackers improve, especially novices.

Selecting a Buck Track

While seemingly simple, finding and selecting a buck to follow presents many challenges to the tracker. The first condition to satisfy is finding snow. I know several aspiring trackers who would not leave the comfort of an area they knew well without snow. There was a location within driving distance that had snow, but because they were unfamiliar with the terrain and roads, they stayed in place. I made a leap forward in my tracking success when I started to chase snow. A tracker can hunt any area well if he has a buck track in front of him. So, drive to snow, wherever it may be.

Small- and medium-sized bucks will leave tracks that are in many ways similar to large doe tracks. It is in the attention to the details of their behavior where you can begin to sort these bucks out from their mothers and sisters in the woods. It takes following a lot of tracks of both bucks and does to get a handle on what is in front of you. Take the collective information provided in the big picture to base a determination. Many things pronounced as gospel are often not true 100 percent of the time. Bucks with good racks, despite advice to the contrary, will ram through very tight cover where it seems like only a slick-headed doe could slide through. This happens when they are being pushed hard or if they have enough desire to chase a doe. They just don't do it regularly.

Become attentive to urine patterns in the snow. A buck dribbles as he walks and the splatter is ahead of his rear feet instead of behind. Look for tarsal gland marks in beds and learn how they smell. Identification of a truly big buck becomes easier; he'll leave sign like no other deer around.

Buck tracks in general have a consistent 2.5- to 3.5-inch-wide track, with a stride length of 22+ inches and a stagger, or width between tracks, of at least four inches. The bigger these numbers get, the larger the buck. This can vary by region. All of this is at a normal pace on flat ground. Things begin to look different when the buck heads up or down hill. Add in rubs, scrapes or antler marks in the snow as he feeds or beds down, and there is a collection of information that means you are tracking a buck. While all of us want to shoot the biggest buck in the woods, if you are new to tracking I recommend taking as many buck tracks as you can to increase your experience. Bigger bucks are certainly easier to follow, but they are often harder to kill because they have more experience. Learning

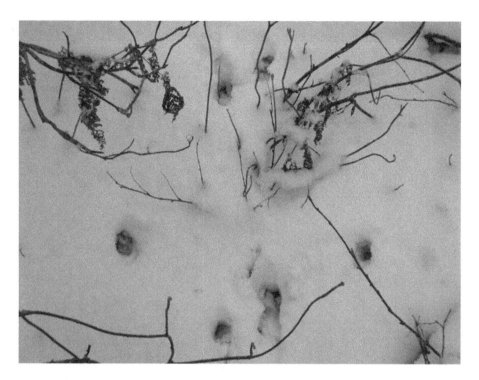

Sign of a doe urinating. Note the splayed feet and urine behind those rear feet imprints.

to track deer and figure out a lot of the nuances requires following deer for quite a while, so get behind one as often as you can. I've also repeatedly taken one buck track and switched to a larger buck in the course of a day. In doing so, I like to make sure that the new track is similarly aged so that not much ground is lost.

How do you find a set of tracks to follow? Most trackers will drive a four-wheel-drive truck into an area, looking for tracks along the way. Some folks will drive around looking all day, others hardly at all. I prefer to have an area picked out that I want to get into in the morning and I look for tracks as I drive in to it. Once there, I park and get in the woods to find a track after daylight. I use preseason scouting to become familiar with the logging road system, the available terrain, recent logging activity and possibly the bucks that are around. With that information, I strike out into the woods to walk in likely areas where bucks might travel. These

This small buck stood to urinate and then stepped in it. He also dribbled as he walked away, which is a classic sign. Some bucks that are traveling won't even stop and you'll see 25 feet of dribble marks.

include mountain saddles, rub and scrape lines, between groups of does and above clear-cuts. Tracking is very much an in the moment activity, so I would rather hunt new, fresh sign over something I learned a month ago or last year. The tracker should be interested in discovering new areas and hunting fresh buck sign in order to be successful.

Sorting Out Tracks

One of the biggest challenges a tracker faces is keeping a buck track sorted out, especially as it twists and turns back on itself or mixes with other deer. Obviously, having a very large-bodied buck with big feet makes this easier but, even still, it can be a challenge to stay alert for the buck ahead of you. Patience in this process is vital. People who try to

Knowing how long your rifle is will help you know how long a step a buck is taking. This Remington 7600 carbine measures 26 inches from the end of the barrel to the back of the trigger guard. Nice step length, not a great stagger.

hurry through often mess it up. I attempt to sort it out by following the buck step for step through the 'barn yard' or by making a loop around the mess of tracks and trying to catch the track coming out. I usually do a combination of both ways depending on the conditions and the particular buck I'm tracking. As I follow the buck into a maze of tracks, I try to stay off his track so I can find it if I have to come back. Working my way through the sign, I pay attention to see if his tracks are headed in multiple directions, in and out, amongst that mess of sign. He might do that while chasing a doe or simply feeding. If he seems to travel straight through I can keep a good pace and get right across; this usually means he was behind the doe group and is trying to catch up to it. If he is with does, he will circle them, scent-check them and if one is ready, chase her

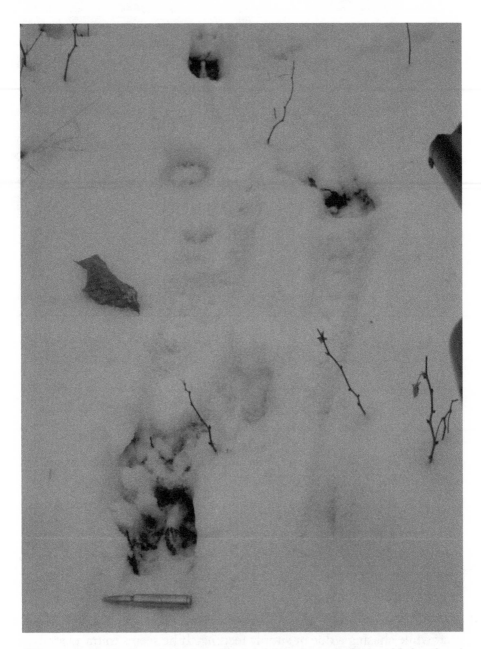

This .30-06 cartridge is 3.25 inches long. This is helpful to know the track width, length and even help estimate the stagger between the tracks.

That saddle in the distance might be a good place to find a buck track.

away from the other deer to try to cut her out of the group and keep her to himself. Depending on the stage of the rut, he may have exited the area with a doe, so care is needed to pick the right set of exiting tracks to follow. Usually there are multiple sets where it looks like he is leaving. I follow each for a while and often he will turn back into the group. If he is making loops in and out of a group of tracks, it is best to swing out around and make a large circle that gets beyond the mess. Hopefully I can find the one spot where he left. Then I just keep tracking. Quite often, I'll see his track leave and return three or four times. I keep making bigger swings until I finally have it straightened out. Tracking with a partner can be a large help. The partner can stay at the last known location and then as I identify tracks, we leapfrog along. This type of situation can become mind numbing and can often give you a tracker's headache, but I have learned a great deal by sticking with it in these tough conditions.

There are a lot of back and forth tracks from several deer here where the deer fed overnight. It is important to take time to sort it out to stay on the buck you are tracking.

I've also learned that when I do screw up a mess of tracks, which I've done regularly, to make sure to go back and sort it out. I have a friend who just gives up on a particular buck if he can't figure things out easily. Opportunities to track a buck are too rare. Learn to take your time and work out those tracks.

Sticking With It

Persistence is one of the biggest factors in becoming a successful buck tracker, maybe the single biggest factor. There isn't anything complicated about this trait: simply show up every day. It is easy to get frustrated and tired as the day and season wear on. Starting each day with a positive outlook goes a long way. Once on a track, plain old hard work often pays off. Being disciplined, dedicated and determined leads to more bucks hanging on the game pole than does wandering around feeling sad or wondering why other guys are lucky. Even after shooting at a buck and missing, it is important to learn those lessons and keep trying. I've seen several guys give up part way through a week of hunting and go home. I know several others who remain around, but their time in the woods gets shorter each day. I understand being tired, but giving up won't put a buck in the bed of the pickup. I find that if I am losing my edge in the woods, it is far better to take a day off to scout or otherwise change it up than it is to quit and go home. Being in shape before the season can help you to grind it out, mentally and physically. All you need is to shoot a buck on the last day once and it will be harder to quit in subsequent seasons.

It is also helpful to have a good hunting partner. I've been lucky to have several guys to hunt with. As my adventures have grown, my father has been willing to come along. We've learned a lot together and keep each other motivated. A good partner will be willing to wait for you after dark, help you drag your buck out and you'll do the same for him (or her). Dad and I double team together on tracks periodically, which is a lot of fun. It contributes to being persistent on a track because we can work it out together. We also got more comfortable being farther out later in the day in more rugged country by being with someone else. Alone is almost always scarier. If you are looking for a hunting partner, find someone that shares the same sense of adventure and style of hunting.

Scouting

Learning to scout in the big woods could be a book by itself. The vast areas of northern timber country don't hold deer that are spread out evenly. The deer there live in pockets. And different than their farm-land brethren, big woods deer don't stay in the same country day-to-day, week-to-week or year-to-year. For the tracker, the purpose of scouting should be to learn if an area holds a big buck. If it does, then scouting shifts to further try to tease out his territory and his travel routes so that he can be found and tracked when there is snow.

Most of this work should be done in late spring or during the fall months when the woods allow sign to be seen. Even during the season if there is bare ground. I recommend starting with maps to identify general areas of interest that are big enough to track a buck through. Then it is vital to at least drive into an area to see what sort of accessibility there is, identify any active or recent logging and maybe even find a track or two on the road. From that point, getting into the woods to find scrape lines, signpost rubs, and likely bedding cover for bucks will start to narrow the areas I want to hunt. I find most of this sign by focusing on how a deer moves around topography first, then logging activity and finally water. If I find sign of a good buck, I like to then try to locate groups of does that he will likely check on through November by focusing on their food sources. This further narrows the area I have to look for the buck when I can track him. This area will still not be small, but it will give me a good idea of where I might be able to cross his path.

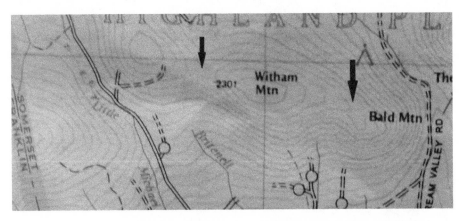

The black arrows indicate saddles that I'd swing through to look for buck sign.

I like to try to locate several good bucks within a road system if I can. I know that their ranges will expand during the rut, but that bucks will often travel similar routes so there will be overlap as they check for does. It can be nice to hang a trail camera to confirm that the buck that I've found is good one, but I don't rely on it. I have found that pictures on a camera will keep me focused on too small an area where a buck may only cruise through once. Also, the woods these bucks move through are big enough that I often won't get a picture of a buck I know is around based on his tracks- I can't realistically run enough cameras.

Things change slightly every year, so it is helpful to check on old areas regularly. Hunting new, up-to-date sign is vastly better than hunting an old area out of habit. On bare ground, it is better and much more fun for me to explore new areas and learn the habits of a new buck. I think it is impossible to have too much knowledge of big bucks to hunt.

Shooting

I needed to improve on several aspects of shooting to be a better and more successful tracker. Learning to shoot quickly, to make shots at running game and considering overall shot selection were important for my growth as a tracker. Having the right set-up for my rifle also led to dragging out more bucks.

A tracker needs to be able to quickly identify his target and get a shot off. A buck coming out of his bed will give you two, maybe three bounds. Attempting to stop that buck with a grunt may lead to a standing shot but that strategy can't be counted on when things are happening quickly in the woods. When there is a shot, it is not likely to be something perfect like on TV. While we should all strive to take the animal down as quickly and as humanely as possible, there are many less-than-textbook shots that will knock a buck down. When there is snow on the ground, getting that buck bleeding will exponentially increase the chances of bringing him down. I've successfully taken bucks with shots at all angles after a lot of practice and consideration. It is vital to carry enough gun, use a strong enough bullet, know anatomy and get a bullet in him. Once I take a shot, I feel I owe it to that animal to see things through all the way to the end, whatever it takes.

Speed and Stealth

Knowing the right speed to track a buck is essential. Del Green, a neighbor of mine, wrote an excellent deer hunting book. In '*Wide Racks and Tall Tales*' he likened the pace of tracking to driving a truck, selecting different gears for different situations. In my mind, the two most important paces are "pretty quick" and "very slow." I have to catch up to that buck, that is the bottom line. Most bucks don't really require running to catch them, but it does have its place. Cruising at a steady, medium speed doesn't serve either end of the hunt well. When I do that, I either don't catch up to the buck or I blow through the stalk. So, moving quickly on the track is the first important step to take. I'd recommend novice trackers haul right along and just keep jumping up deer at first, like I did. I don't recommend you do it for as long as I did though!

Once I got to where I was seeing a lot of white tails bouncing ahead of me in the woods, I learned to slow down and go deathly slow. Key indicators to slow down include a shift to a meandering pace, evidence of heavy feeding, and a change of direction uphill. If the buck I am tracking is making a lot of rubs and scrapes between groups of does I also feel I should be able to catch up with him. When I see that sign and think he is close, I stop hunting with my feet and start hunting with my eyes. I try to be on red alert with intense focus on seeing that buck in a wide arc ahead of me. Try to approach open areas so that you remain in the cover to spot him in the hard woods or clear cut in front of you. Treat ridges the same way, so that as you crest them you are scanning before you reveal yourself.

Along with speed, I had to work on being stealthy. Sneaking in on a buck requires attention to detail and great focus. I learned how to step quietly and not shift my weight until I knew I wouldn't break a branch. I began to slide my body around branches that might break or leaves that would rustle. I had to reduce noise and movement to limit things that would give me away. Over time, I stopped grabbing saplings that would shake ten feet over my head, emptied the keys and change out of my pockets and got rid of noisy clothes and water bottles. The terrain and snow conditions, along with what the buck is doing in front of you will dictate just how fast or how slow to go, but going slow enough is the key to getting a shot at him.

Other Skills

There are a few other basic skills that I think helped my success climb. One is to get away from other hunters. Find remote or overlooked areas that are hard to access. Access might be limited by a gate, a nasty river crossing or steep terrain that other people may not want to tackle. Most people don't like to get more than one mountain away from their truck, so being willing to get deeper into the country is effective in having more country to yourself. Get good gear and know how to use it. This includes wool clothing, good boots, GPS (covered in the next chapter). Learn how to read a topo map and identify key areas like saddles, swamps and mountain tops. Also learn to see roads and identify stretches of country that are far from them.

Another must is to have good basic woodsmanship skills. These skills can often be worked on by hunting small game. I like to jump shoot grouse in the fall without the aid of a dog while I'm scouting. In the winter months I like to chase snowshoe hare, again without a dog. Not enough people hunt small game anymore and the skills learned on these small, tasty animals translate directly to tracking deer. The time spent hunting small game can also be used to learn and expand the knowledge of other skills like how to start a fire in less than ideal conditions, learning how to use a map and compass to navigate when the GPS dies and achieving a basic level of comfort while moving around in the woods. Figuring out how to cross brooks and swamps, finding good paths through thick growth and how to navigate a mountain will increase the enjoyment of being out there. I also want a vehicle I can trust to get me out and back. I carry along equipment that I know how to use to extricate the truck should I get it stuck. These skills breed confidence to stay in the woods with my focus entirely on the buck ahead of me.

Common Pitfalls

Paralleling these keys to success are some common pitfalls that I have suffered through as an aspiring tracker. For me, these challenges are not mastered just once, but tend to pop up repeatedly. I like to remind myself of these things before the season to try to avoid having to relearn them after I've screwed something up. I've lumped them into three big categories that have lots of smaller pieces within them.

The first pitfall is thinking too small. This holds true on a number of levels. The first is the terrain I want to get into. I used to try to track a deer in a half-mile square block of woods and he'd either cross onto posted property or someone else would take his track. I've learned that I want to find big areas, as devoid of roads as possible. It isn't that small areas don't hold big bucks, but rather that I want to roam without crossing roads or running into other people. I also used to make a very specific plan to get to a certain point on a map and then hunt directly to it. While this got me where I wanted to go, I found more sign and better hunting if I covered a wider slice of the country. This means looking around more within the area I'm hunting. There might not be buck sign in one spot, but there might be 300 yards away. Lastly, I used to follow any deer track I came across. Then I started to tease out which ones were bucks, which was a step forward, but a small buck can be tough to follow when he mixes with similar sized does. It is better to leave smaller tracks alone and get a little more selective with a bigger buck track. Think big.

The second pitfall I used to fall prey to is not being fully committed to tracking. This lack of commitment often had more to do with all the extracurricular things that go on during deer season. I had times where I would get worn out before the best tracking snow came. I might have bow hunted too much in October or run around on bare ground many days in a row, getting tired when there was snow in the forecast. Even things like having too much fun at camp could impact both my day-to-day focus as well as my ability to intensely focus on tracking across the entirety of a six week season. It isn't that these fun things shouldn't happen, but rather how I chose to fit them in and recover from them so that I could be ready to go hard when conditions were right. Fully commit to being a deer tracker.

The last pitfall category is thinking too much. I'm a planner and a thinker. This often gets in the way. I used to have a cabin booked months in advance of deer season without knowing what would be going on in terms of snow or buck sign. This thinking would drift into my daily hunting. I'd wonder about work issues, what Dad was up to, where I'd be hunting tomorrow or if I was in the right spot today. Things like fear could distract me too. Could I get back to the truck by dark or where was I in the woods? All those thoughts diverted my attention away from the task at hand. The goal is to be completely in the moment when tracking a buck. That might require some details taken care of early, so that everything else in life is squared away. It also meant learning to quiet the noise in my head down and resolving fear. In this era of information overload from internet and social media that can be a tall task, but the more I stay present when tracking a buck, the less I miss and the better I do. Keep it simple- find a buck, track him and kill him. Don't overthink it.

All of these keys to success and common pitfalls tend to overlap and blend together for a buck tracker. As I've become persistent enough to sort out a barnyard of tracks, I also became more likely to stay on a track all day. Each day I hunt is part of a larger educational experience that is enhanced by working to hone these skills in the woods. I started to think not just about the buck I tracked that day but about what I gained in terms of knowledge and experience for a tracking adventure down the road.

Chapter 9

GEAR

As we progress as trackers, our gear improves. When I started following my father around in the woods in the early 1980s, I wore blue jeans, moon boots and a winter coat – not the stealthiest or warmest attire. When my feet got wet, which they inevitably did, we would often go back to camp, change our cotton socks, put bread bags on our feet and get back out there. As time passed my gear has improved, yet it is difficult to stay on top of what works best. I believe a deer hunter is built from the ground up, whether that is training or gear, so we'll start with boots and work up from there.

Boots and Socks

The wet areas I hunt require rubber boots that are high enough to allow me to ford good-sized streams. If the stream is higher than the tops and I need to get across, I'll strip down and wade. On one recent hunt, I parked then wanted to cross a river to get into a good area from a different direction. There was a skiff of snow on the ground and it had rained, so the river was higher than normal and I couldn't find a place to cross within a tenth of a mile up or downstream. So I staged myself at the truck, got undressed, then headed across. As I put my clothes back on, unfortunately I was one sock short. Keys in hand, I stripped back down, went back across and located my sock. Finally dressed, I proceeded on my hunt, warming up quickly. Unfortunately, my dreams of crossing the river dragging a buck on my way out did not materialize. My boots are generally uninsulated because I hunt on the move and wear good wool socks. I wear Lacrosse Alpha Burly boots and Darn Tough wool socks. I usually place a wool arch support made by Superfeet in my boots. I like those rubber boots because of their aggressive tread and stiffer sole that make mountains more comfortable to climb than other boots. I want the waterproof features of a rubber boot because the New England terrain is pretty wet. Darn Tough over-the-calf socks are warm and wear very well. The wool arch support adds some insulation and support under my foot, which is where I first get cold. I always have a PEET boot dryer at home (or in camp) so I can get the sweat inside my boots to dry out overnight.

Darn Tough over-the-calf socks and Smartwool compression sleeves keep my feet warm and feeling good. I hate when my socks slide down.

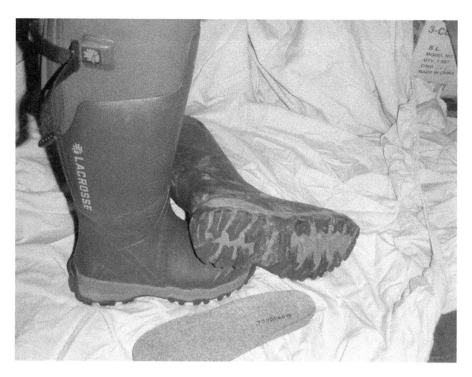

Rubber boots and some supportive Superfeet insoles keep me moving.

Wool Clothes

The old, now-discontinued Beaglewear was great for outerwear and now the Big Woods Bucks pants and jacket made by Silent Predator rivals it. Wool is quiet, water resistant, it retains its warmth when wet and is naturally scent reducing due to its natural antimicrobial properties. I wear both pants and a jacket made of wool throughout the season. Typically I wear suspenders to hold the pants up. My pants pockets are standard, no cargo pockets needed. I keep a folding compass with a small mirror in one pocket, extra shells in another, my license in a rear pocket and some paper towels. My knife is secured in a sheath and hangs off my suspenders. My jacket holds my GPS, rifle sling, a pin-on compass and my gloves. I hunt with wool gloves made by Fox River and I use full fingered or fingerless depending on the weather and how fast I'm

Wool Pants, Jacket, Vest, Hat, GPS, Pin-on and regular compasses as well as Chapstick. A knife on my suspenders and some paper towels (for various purposes) makes up my outerwear for tracking.

moving. My hat is a blaze orange Gore-Tex cap I purchased through Cabela's or a Stormy Kromer if it gets colder than 20°F. There are many modern options for clothing, but most don't combine the quietness and insulating properties of wool that are most effective on a day to day basis.

Layering is really how to modify clothing for the weather. My undergarments are made of wool as well, usually Merino wool by First Lite. They manufacture boxer briefs, long johns, t-shirts and long-sleeve long underwear that I mix and match depending on the day. A couple pairs of each will work for a week. Even if I sweat I can get two or three days out of a set of their clothing without feeling like my scent is a concern. While tracking, the wind can blow from all directions in the course of a day and, while the deer react to scent, I don't believe it is their primary

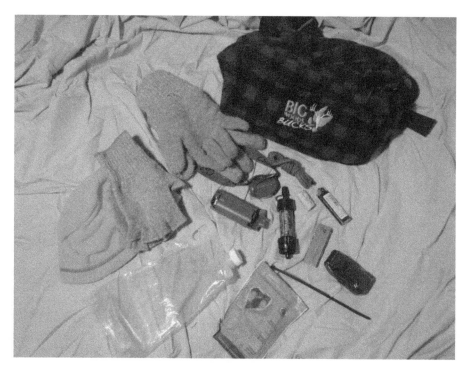

Fanny pack and basic supplies for a day of hunting.

defense. While you should attempt to keep foreign odors minimized, I don't believe you need to go to extremes regarding scent control. It is more important to have clothing that keeps you comfortable and quiet.

Other Gear

The rest of my gear, other than my rifle, lives in my 450 cubic inch wool fanny pack. The fanny pack, sold by Big Woods Bucks, is quiet and big enough for my gear. Similar versions are sold by Johnson. I use a Platypus one-liter bottle for water that I can squeeze air out of as I drink so it doesn't slosh. I carry a grunt call around my neck. My food items go in there, usually a sandwich, apple and a bar of some sort, along with spare GPS batteries, a small digital camera, a drag rope, a couple zip ties, a space blanket, two ways to start a fire (lighter and waterproof matches),

My rifle line up. From top to bottom: Peep-sighted Rem 760 carbine in .30-06, Thompson Center Triumph in .50 cal, Rem 7600 carbine .30-06 with Redfield 2-7x, Browning X-Bolt .30-06 (for western hunting). Also included is a 1 inch nylon sling. 90% of my hunting is done with middle two, which also have peep sight backups with quick release mounts.

another 4 rounds of ammo, extra gloves, a wool, blaze-orange tuque, and a water purifier.

This setup will allow me to spend the night in the woods in almost any conditions. I had an unplanned night in the woods while on an elk hunt in Colorado that led me to add the space blanket and water purifier to my daily list. They are more than worth their weight. Most of these items have multiple uses, both daily and in an emergency. For example, you can tag your deer with a zip tie or use one to secure your space blanket over a pole to make a shelter.

My rifle can vary on the season and conditions. I typically carry a Remington 7600 carbine in .30-06 during rifle seasons, but have also carried bolt actions and semi-autos and shot deer with them. Calibers

The gear that is stowed in the box in the bed of my truck. There is a collapsible shovel in the bucket along with several ropes, straps, and miscellaneous items.

have included 7mm-08, 7mm Rem. Mag., .30-06 and .44 Rem. Mag. I've used peep sights, but now primarily keep a 2-7x Redfield Revolution scope on most of my rifles, mounted on a rail with Leopold Quick Release Mounts. I have a peep back up for the 7600, as well as for my Thompson Center Triumph .50 cal. muzzleloader. Rifles have sling mounts, but I typically only use the sling when walking a road in or out of the woods or when dragging a deer.

I keep backups of most of these items at the truck, along with extra food and drinks, another shirt and pair or two of socks for anyone to use. I like to change into my rubber boots just before hunting so I have a spare pair of boots at the truck as well. My truck is a regular four wheel drive. I'm not mechanically inclined, so I haven't lifted it or done anything special. I get my mechanic to go through it just before the season. I do try to make sure the trucks I buy now have skid plates underneath and I generally put 10 ply tires on them to lessen the likelihood of a puncture on the old logging roads I travel. I've thought about buying tires chains for icy roads, but have been ok without them for the last decade. I just drive until I can't anymore and hunt on foot from there. Don't let the lack of a woods-ready vehicle stop you. My first buck was loaded onto an old Ford Escort hatchback! There is usually a map of where we are hunting in the truck for reference. In a box in the bed of the truck I carry a chainsaw, medical kit, tarp, extra fuel and oil, a portable booster pack with air compressor, shovel, and a come-along with synthetic rope for minor vehicle mishaps. If something major happens, we'll hoof it out until we get a ride and then figure things out.

Gear choices are very personal but you should choose items that serve multiple uses, are reliable, and get the job done. Things go on and off this list regularly, and I try to keep what I carry to a minimum.

Chapter 10

PRESEASON TRAINING

THE tracking season is brief and intense. With dedication and the right job, you might hunt for four to six weeks. Of all those days, if you are lucky, you might have three excellent days for tracking and another six to eight mediocre days with snow on the ground. That's the best-case scenario as the climate changes, in my experience over the last decade. Some years there may be even less opportunity. Most of us only get a week or two off per year, leaving us with hit or miss conditions. With that in mind, you definitely want to hit the ground running in order to track down your buck. You don't want to be in poor shape when the time comes. To be at your best it is important to prepare ahead of the season. This means you have your gear set, physical training completed, mental attitude properly adjusted and shooting skills practiced. All these things can and should be tailored to your individual needs so that you can execute at a high level when the snow hits. Then all that is left to worry about is tracking.

Physical Preparation

I like to break down the physical demands of tracking into three components: daily endurance, season endurance and strength. Daily endurance is how far you can go on a particular day. The demand might be as high as 15 miles in one day.

Season endurance is how you can keep up that mileage day after day, all season long. Part of the challenge is how well you do with little sleep and altered nutrition.

Lastly, general strength includes ensuring your legs get you up a mountain, your arms carry a seven-pound rifle all week and having the power to drag your buck a mile out of the woods to the nearest road.

These three components play into one another, along with intangibles like mental toughness and grit, to produce an overall capacity for this aggressive form of hunting. Trackers, much like Western backcountry hunters, need to be able to cover relatively long distances (five or more miles on average) on a daily basis and then get themselves, and hopefully a buck, out of the woods. We need to be able to repeat that for five or six days per week for up to six weeks. The math on that is impressive, up around 180 miles. During the 2016 season I hunted 29 days and estimate that I walked 160 miles. I gained and lost significant elevation as well. I shot my second buck of the year on the second-to-last day of the season, dragged him out and loaded him in the truck. That buck, dressed out, weighed more than me.

I can get pretty geeky when it comes to training for hunting. I'm a physical therapist, so exercise fits into my life. I've come to realize most people don't get excited talking about training like I do. Instead, they want to increase their fitness level with a relatively small investment of time and energy. To that end, I've created a plan that should deliver reasonable results. I'll outline some basics. I encourage you to get in as good a shape as possible to hunt hard and well all-season long.

Many people start the conversation with me about getting prepared to hunt by expressing a desire to lose some weight. I think this is an important factor, particularly as we age. About 80 percent of weight loss is related to our eating habits. Change those habits and you can lose weight. This should be a lifestyle change and not a short-term diet. Most people know what a good diet looks like, they just don't follow it. Not being a nutritionist and realizing that everyone has different needs, I'll keep my recommendations very general:

- Eat primarily real food: fruits, vegetables, meat and fish.
- Keep portion sizes reasonable.
- Limit intake of excess sugar and processed grains.

The other 20 percent of weight loss will come from exercise and other factors, mostly related to a healthier lifestyle that includes good sleep. Eat well, exercise, drink water and get good sleep.

Injuries

It is important to not get hurt while training, so back off a bit if things feel more serious than run-of-the-mill discomfort when exercising. I see many people in my clinic who try to make fitness gains in one month that really take a year. Training is an investment in your body, so it pays to think long term. Progress slowly over time and accumulate a lot of small gains. Ben Franklin was right when he noted that "An ounce of prevention is worth a pound of cure."

In each session there is potential for harm. To minimize this, I recommend a gradual warm up into your activity to start. There is mixed evidence about the benefits of stretching before activity for preventing injury. In light of that, light stretching or yoga should take place after your training is done. You should address any long-term injuries or problems in the offseason, rather than ignoring them until the hunting season is upon you. I always get a guy in my clinic in October who wants his leg pain better in four weeks, even though it has been bothering him for the last nine months. That isn't going to happen. Get things looked at in January rather than waiting until the fall.

Timeline

From an exercise standpoint, most people make a lot of gains over about 12 weeks of a program, then those gains start to tail off and the fitness level plateaus. To really make progress, you have to start training harder. This is known as the law of diminishing returns. An Olympic athlete trying to win a gold medal wants to eke out every ounce of progress they can, so working into that area of diminishing returns makes sense. For a buck tracker, shaving a quarter of a second off your 100-meter sprint time isn't really beneficial. I recommend getting the big gains, then shifting into a different training phase. For the hunter who has a demanding hunt on the calendar, especially tackling a big Western or Alaskan hunt, I recommend a 12 month or more commitment to fitness. For the average northern tracker, two, eight to twelve-week cycles of training will make you a more effective predator in the woods without getting overwhelmed. I label these cycles as general training and hunt-specific training.

General Training

Starting 16-24 weeks before the anticipated hunting season, an aspiring tracker will want to start preparing for the rigors of the hunt. You should gradually ramp up the effort level throughout this phase. In general, it is best to exercise four or five days per week and get some rest on the off days. The components of this program are four days of walking and two days of strengthening.

Cardiovascular training should take place four days per week. Walking is great. Some guys will run and others may prefer an elliptical trainer, a rowing machine or a bike. It really doesn't matter; do what is best for your body. There is probably some benefit in mixing it up to avoid any overuse injuries. On the four days that you perform your cardio exercise, make one a long day, one day a medium day and two days short. These are relative terms, but in general, a long effort would be around a 60- to 90-minute walk, the medium effort 40-60 minutes and the short efforts 20-40 minutes. The pace should be self-selected; you want to breathe hard and sweat but be able to complete the effort without feeling completely exhausted. Longer effort should be completed at a slower pace than the medium and shorter efforts. Over the course of the eight- to twelve-week program, you should notice that you can go further and/or faster for a given effort as your fitness increases.

Running is one way to get your heart and lungs ready for hunting. There are many other good options like biking, hiking and swimming if running isn't your thing.

Strength training in this period should be focused on making gains in bodyweight activities like lunges, push-ups, pull-ups and core strengthening. These exercises should take place two days a week. They often fit in nicely on the short cardiovascular effort days but can be completed separately. In general, start with two sets of five to eight repetitions of each exercise and build up gradually until you can complete three sets of 12-15 reps. Form should be excellent with strengthening exercises; if you are unsure how to perform them, I suggest consulting with a professional strength coach.

The Lunge is a great general training exercise.

Hunt-Specific Training

In this second period of training, it's time to get specific to the demands of hunting. This eight- to twelve-week training cycle will continue to focus on cardiovascular endurance with more specific strength training added in. In terms of scheduling, plan on taking about a week off before your hunting season begins for overall recovery. You don't want to have sore quads the first day going up a mountain. Plan on exercising five or six days per week; four days of cardiovascular activity overlapped with two or three days of strength training and then one separate day of "hunt effort" activity.

The four days of cardiovascular training will be the same – long, medium and short efforts –except they will be longer. I recommend that the bulk of these efforts be walking or hiking to more specifically mimic the demands of the hunt. I've never tracked a buck down on the stair climber! Generally, any training is better than none, so do what you can. The long effort should now be 90-120 minutes in length, the medium effort will be 45-90 minutes and the two shorter efforts will be 30-45 minutes in length. I recommend the addition of a pack with weight if you are walking for your training. Start with 10 pounds in your pack and increase a little each week. Wear boots when you can. I generally train in my Western hunting boots as they weigh more and I need to break them in. I do not train in my rubber boots because my feet sweat too much in them and they break down too quickly. I do use the same foot bed in both types of boots though, so my feet adapt to that support.

Hiking with weight in a pack is an excellent way to get in shape before your hunting adventure.

The strength training progression in this phase is about adding some weight to previous exercises, as well as incorporating a few specific exercises. I recommend wearing a pack or using a sandbag while doing lunges at this time. Start with a weight that feels challenging for two sets of eight and build up to the three sets of 15 reps before increasing the weight. I recommend adding in the hinge lift (also known as the dead-lift) during this training period. Additional exercises I like to include are the log drag and suitcase carry. In New England, we tend to drag our deer out, which is a high demand activity that can cause problems if we are not prepared. People have experienced heart attacks or suffered other injuries dragging out their buck. To prepare, I like to drag a big log around my yard. For the suitcase carry, get a heavy weight or five gallon pail of water or sand and walk around with it for the specified time in each hand. This will prepare your back and shoulders for carrying your rifle and other unbalanced activities. For both of these exercises, I typically start with three sets of 30 seconds in my three weekly sessions, and then build up to five sets of two minutes before the season arrives. The total active time, ten minutes, doesn't come anywhere close to the time spent carrying a rifle, nor does it simulate what it takes to drag a buck out, but it does familiarize my body and my mind with the effort required so that there is no shock when I start to lug my rifle around for eight hours or when I tie that rope to his antlers and begin pulling.

Lastly, as part of this training period, I recommend what I call a "hunt-effort activity." Usually this amounts to a long hike with a pack on for greater than two hours. This can be a specific training hike or part of a larger scouting or bird hunting trip in the fall. The point is to work on your long effort tolerance, under load, in hunting conditions. This is best done in the woods, on a trail hike that is not smooth, can also be beneficial. If you lack a sufficient trail in terms of steepness or terrain, you can do repeats up and down a steep bank or stairs to simulate this effort.

The intent of this program is to prepare for the rigors of tracking in the big woods, as well as dragging your buck out. I assumed you will shoot your buck on the last hour of the last day of your six-day hunt. There is no such thing as being over prepared. If your hunt seems too easy after six days climbing mountains and slogging through swamps and you have

The log drag helps prepare me for dragging a buck out of the woods.

a big buck in the back of your truck, good for you. When things get hard with training, think back to past hunts, recall the buck you couldn't catch up to and learn how to just keep going.

Physical Training Summary

- Train for endurance first, then strength.

- Cardiovascular endurance is developed by activity that has you moving over ground, breathing hard, and sweating for 40 minutes, five days per week.

- Lift weights in functional movements like hinge, squat, push and pull.

- Two days a week will get you stronger in a range of five sets of five at a challenging but doable level.

Mental Preparation

Mental and physical fitness are tangled together. They exist in harmony to act both as a safety mechanism, so that the body is not pushed far beyond its limits, and as a performance enhancer, where the body does things that were once unimaginable. How are these seemingly opposite outcomes possible from one source? I think it has to do with developing the right attitude and then building mental toughness. When both these factors are high, the mind acts to push the body to new heights of performance. When attitude and toughness slip, the mind shuts the body down. Thankfully, these traits improve with effort and training.

Tracking deer is an endurance activity, so I like to look to the endurance sports world for corollaries. Some people just seem to have a little more grit, a little more persistence in the face of tough odds. It seems to be inborn, like the color of your eyes or the size of your feet. The people who seem gifted with this ability are often rewarded for their extra effort. They occasionally suffer from it as well, pushing the limits and putting themselves and others in dangerous situations. The divide between the extremes of success and suffering is a thin one, but most of us never even begin to approach that line. We would accomplish more of our goals in hunting, and life, if we pushed toward it a bit more.

Rather than a purely inherited trait, mental toughness is a skill that can be learned and improved upon by training. It is often enhanced by physical training and life experience. People who have suffered and persevered to achieve their goals usually gain a sense of perspective that what they are going through now is not that much worse than what they've been through in the past. For example, elite runners who come out of a particular tribe in Kenya to win marathons, learn to suffer in the transition from adolescence to adulthood. The males of the tribe undergo circumcision and are forced to run everywhere in the month following. Talk about a physical ordeal! This painful process teaches these tribesmen to manage pain and endure, a lesson they learn well and then apply to the suffering they feel when racing. In our society, pain and failure are kept to a minimum. So many of us have no idea how to manage in the face of discomfort or disappointment.

Do we need to undergo a painful ritual to succeed as trackers? No. But a mental edge can be the difference between filling a tag and driving an empty truck out of the woods, dejected. Taken to its extreme, mental toughness can also help us in survival situations, where command of attitude and motivation can spell the difference between life and death.

A positive attitude is essential. Belief that you will track that buck down, that you will make a good shot, that you will survive a night in the woods sets an expectation for the mind to put forth the required effort. Similar to a race, if you are in second place and don't believe you can catch the frontrunner, you definitely won't. The right attitude is easy to achieve on the first day of hunting season, harder to maintain through the last day. Waking up each morning believing "today is the day!" is essential for a tracker. When it ends up not happening, taking that disappointment in stride and looking at it in a positive light will help set the stage for a positive start to the next day. I like to review the day and figure out what I did poorly and then work to improve upon it. I've tracked and killed enough late season bucks to believe my chances are as good on the last day as they are on the first.

The proper attitude and mental toughness can be developed by graded exposure to tough circumstances. These techniques are just a small example of ways to challenge yourself; you can find your own way to develop the right attitude. I like to train the very things that often make people quit during the season: being tired, wet or cold. These are the same variables the military uses to challenge recruits. I train for them in small, safe doses and recommend you do the same. You should even check with your doctor.

One tactic for developing a tolerance to cold is to spend 30-60 seconds at the end of your shower with no hot water. The shock will initially cause you to lose your breath, but eventually your system will remain calm and you can breathe through it. I also like to go out and start my truck without a coat on all winter. Some mornings that might be a -20°

experience, but you will notice that you get used to it. You should be careful with this; a number of years ago I ended up locking myself out of my apartment and out of my car with just a t-shirt on; luckily the store across the street was open. Learned a lesson from that little event as well! I also try to get in the lake near my house for as many months as the water is open. I have someone with me when this gets extreme. I usually end up in the water from April through November.

Fatigue is also a factor to manage, so I like to get up early in the morning for my exercise. Training in the dark while the rest of the world is sleeping can give you a feeling of toughness. The same is true by training late at night. Pick something you are not good at or dislike and work on it. Figure out a way to do things others won't, so that when the time comes, you will be able to do the things that they can't.

Shooting Preparation

Shooting has been my Achilles' heel. I sometimes wonder what my wall would like if I traded in the bucks I've missed for the ones I've hit. There are any number of reasons and excuses why I've shot poorly in the past: I've used sights that weren't set up properly or ideal for me, I've thought too much or too little about a shot, I've hesitated a split second too long or taken the shot too quickly. Buck fever never comes to mind as an excuse; I don't really lose my mind at the moment, I just execute poorly. I have an uncle, who hasn't shot many deer, that once ejected every shell from his bolt-action rifle without actually pulling the trigger at a nearby buck, swearing he was shooting at him until his son picked up the still-full casings. That is buck fever. Thankfully, regardless of how good or poor a shot we are, shooting is a learned skill that we can improve upon. On the plus side, all of that missing means I'm getting close to these bucks, right?

The first part of shooting preparation is getting your game eye developed. A tracker needs to learn to spot game. Not whole animals, but pieces and parts. Every minute in the woods is an opportunity to practice spotting game. I had to learn to pick out an ear flicker and a head turning with my peripheral vision. Some of the process is learning to look *for* something rather than *at* something. Once I spotted my first bedded deer, I knew where and what to look for, so spotting others became easier. That peripheral vision is important because most of the time the deer will be off to one side or the other. After game is spotted, making the shot comes next.

You can choose whatever rifle and sight set up you like, just make sure it fits you and that you can use it well. I recommend hunting with only one rifle every season. If you want to switch it up, do so over the summer so you can hunt with the new rig that fall. You also need to select good bullets that your rifle shoots accurately. It is hard to go wrong these days, as most modern bullets are well constructed. For New England with my .30-06, shooting 180 grain bullets, I like to sight in from the bench dead on at 100 yards. Most shots are going to be close and quick, so I use a relatively low power, variable scope, 2x-7x. It has an Accu-range reticle made by Redfield that places a circle around the crosshairs to make for quick point-and-shoot. Once I've sighted in, I don't use a bench except to check my zero periodically.

Mounting the rifle quickly, acquiring the target and pulling the trigger in the time it takes a buck to get up from his bed and make two bounds is the goal for the tracker. Practice for this starts at home, well before the season. With a rifle that you know is unloaded, pick a random knot on a tree and pull up, centering the crosshairs on that knot. Bring the rifle down and repeat. Make this as realistic as possible by wearing your hunting coat, especially as the season approaches. Make sure the knot is not always directly in front of you, but off to either side as well. As you get faster and more efficient, begin to pull the trigger and work the action. Use a dummy round if you feel it is better for the firing mechanism. I've heard that it doesn't hurt a modern rifle to dry fire it, but you should find out for your specific gun. I recommend home drills at least 30 mounts of the rifle, twice per week. It is also helpful to study deer anatomy at home, so that you have an understanding of where you are trying to place that bullet and where the various lethal areas on a deer exist. Look at a variety of pictures of deer at all angles, standing, bedded, and various quartering and straight on or away to plan for shot opportunities.

At the range, you'll want to work through drills specific to shooting while tracking. I start with shooting paper bullseye targets regularly at known distances in the standard offhand position. I then supplement with a couple of other drills. With all these drills the goal is to get faster and maintain accuracy, so I start slowly and deliberately and work my way up. If I try to get too fast, I notice my accuracy suffers. I like to set up several targets at various distances out to 100 yards and shoot quickly from one to the next. Practice moving left to right, right to left, near to far and far to near from target to target to simulate a deer moving. If I have a partner with me, we will often set up targets at variable distances with different colors and then stand facing right or left. The partner will then call out a color and you have to react quickly to this and shoot that target. It is important to unlearn or avoid developing any bad habits, like flinching or pulling your cheek off the rifle stock. A good way to do this is to run through a number of shots and drills with a .22 that you have set up similarly to your deer hunting rifle. I hunt with a Remington 7600 pump and have a Remington 572 pump to practice with. Both go the range with me regularly and I try to shoot the .22 at least twice as much as the .30-06.

There are a couple other ways to get better at the moving target aspect often encountered while tracking. One is rolling tire practice, where a tire is rolled off a hill into range and you must swing with it and get your shots off. You can also tie a balloon to a string with a light weight on it so that it bounces along in the breeze. You learn to pick your shots at that inconsistently moving target. I find shooting skeet in the summer to be good practice as well. I just recommend you start every station with the shotgun in the ready position, as opposed to mounted on the shoulder, before you call "pull." This will make mounting part of a smoother overall process. I use a pump shotgun in this scenario. My score suffers a bit, but my deer shooting improves.

Shooting at rolling tires is good practice for running shots.

With all shooting, safety is of course paramount. Wear hearing protection and eye protection. Follow range rules and double check everything. I even wear a shoulder pad to keep a flinch from developing. I try to go to the range once every other week or so, though it bumps up a little as the season approaches. I don't shoot a lot when I'm there, maybe eight rounds out of my .30-06 and twice that out of my .22. I try to be very deliberate in my practice. Repetition will make things automatic, so find a way to get that rifle to your shoulder as much as you can before the season. It is a good idea to stay sharp in the season as well. A shot here or there is helpful to keep the zero checked. I try to pull up on every grouse that startles me and get it in the scope as quickly as possible. Learning to shoot well under field conditions will help you immensely while tracking. Don't assume you are a natural. I never believe anyone who tells me they shoot better at a deer than they do at the range; that is usually luck. What if you've never missed a deer? Well, I'd guess that you haven't shot at enough of them.

Chapter 11

GROUND TO TABLE

A shift in our culture in recent years has seen more people desire local
food. There are multiple reasons for this attitude, as numerous as
the individuals wanting to make a change in how they source their food.
Common thoughts include a move away from industrial food produc-
tion to something more sustainable, an urge to have a deeper connection
with food and where it comes from, as well as health benefits. Hunting
for meat satisfies all these desires. A buck shot near your home is as sustainable and local as it gets. I can't think of a healthier source of protein
than a wilderness deer. But many people are unaware of the proper steps
to produce quality meat to enjoy through the coming months. Every
meal you make out of your buck will bring back memories of the hunt as
enjoyable as looking at a rack on the wall.

Creating good meat starts as soon as the buck is on the ground. The
less stressful his last moments are before being killed, the more likely his
meat is going to be tender – though some bucks that I've had to chase
still turned out just fine. A deer that dies quickly with minimal stress
is thought to produce less adrenaline and have less tension within his
muscles. These factors are thought to produce better flavors and texture
of meat. A gut shot animal that lives for a while after the shot can have
some of the bacteria of its gut taint the flavor. Some of these things can
be mitigated by proper care.

Once the deer is down, I take a few quiet moments to reflect on the
occasion and thank him for the chase. Having tracked the buck, I experience an intimacy in the relationship that I don't feel in other forms

of hunting. Whatever your belief system, taking a life is not a trivial experience. It is okay to cry, laugh, hoot or simply be somber. Waves of emotion will accompany this moment, especially for an inexperienced hunter. These emotions will mellow and mature with time, with softening edges and an acceptance of the task's gravity settling in. Life sustains life; it always has and it always will. A sense that you are more intimately involved with your food and with the world around you takes over. You won't be able to imagine any better way to fill your freezer.

I recommend taking a few good pictures before gutting you buck. I carry a small digital camera with an automatic timer feature. A small, flexible tripod can be helpful. Often I just find a log to set the camera on. Wipe up obvious blood if you can, tuck his tongue in his mouth and make sure the buck is the focus of the picture. I personally don't use any tricks designed to present anything other than the truth. I see a lot of folks holding antlers at arm's length or sitting far back from the deer to create the effect of a larger set of antlers. This is unnecessary. You are who you are and the buck is who he is, so let the picture be honest. The trophy, after all, is in the story you wrote to get there. Once I take a few pictures, the task of truly making meat begins.

To make the process safe, be sure to take your time and be systematic. Following specific rules of the state I am hunting, I'll tag the buck. I then start by taking off my blaze orange jacket and hat and hang them where they can be seen from a distance. I roll up my sleeves and set aside my fanny pack, opening it up so I don't have to fool around with zippers with bloody hands. I pull out paper towels if I have some and set them where I can access them. I pull out my folding knife with a blade that is about three inches long and locks straight.

Getting the buck on his back with his head slightly uphill if I can, I stand over his chest facing his hind end. I usually try to hold the chest still between my legs. I find the bottom of the sternum and cut slowly through the hair and skin there, making a cut down through the tissue until I know I am at the layer of muscle that holds in the abdominal contents. I skin down to between the legs to the pelvic bone without getting deep into the cavity. I then carefully return to my starting point and cut through this muscle and expose the guts. Keeping the point of the knife headed away from me with the sharp edge up, I reach two fingers of my left hand in between the layers of tissue and guts then lift, allowing me to slide the knife in and cut through the skin. I work my way down as far as I can, keeping the body steady between my legs. When I arrive where the deer's legs are in the way, I'll use my legs to stabilize them open. I try to avoid touching his tarsal glands. I cut around the penis and scrotum down to the pelvis, paying attention not to cut the ureter. I then turn around and make a full cut around the anus, trying to free up all the tissue connections in there. Once done, I reach up and haul out the guts. There are numerous tissue connections within the abdomen that will need to be freed up with the knife as you remove the contents of the abdomen. Go slowly here as this can result in a cut and an infection if you are not paying attention. Some folks wear gloves during this process. I usually have to work to free up things within that boney cavity so that the anus and large intestine can come out whole. I take care to not get urine on the meat of the exposed hindquarter.

Once the abdomen is cleared, I cut through the diaphragm into the chest cavity. I reach up as far as I can to sever the windpipe and esophagus, making sure to take the heart out as well. These are blind movements with the knife so, again, be careful not to cut yourself. There will be a lot of blood still in the cavity, so it might be helpful to shift the deer around and get the deer oriented so that some blood can drain out down through the abdomen and pelvic openings, giving you a clear view. At this point, you are essentially done. If you like to eat liver and heart be sure to grab those organs and put them in a bag or back in the chest cavity for the drag out. I usually try to clean myself up with snow or a nearby stream, wiping off with paper towels. I also make sure to find my knife, as I have left more than one in the woods after setting it aside.

For dragging the deer to the truck, I carry a five-foot length of rope. I can usually find a strong branch close by that I break off to a length of about 18-24 inches. I wrap the rope around the base of the antlers and tie a knot, then shorten the rope so that, when I'm dragging, his head is off the ground. I tie it to my drag stick at that point. I then make a half hitch with the rope around his nose so that when I lift, his head is in line with the dragging connection and is less likely to get hung up on trees and branches as I slide him through the woods. I try to drag him out of the woods by the best route I can find. Blown down trees and dense cover can make it quite challenging. Uphill is always hard! Some drags are easy and some stink. It is a job that just needs to get done. But it does not need to be done quickly. Take a lot of breaks and go easy; this is when people hurt themselves or get into trouble with their hearts from pushing themselves too hard.

Dragging a buck out is a labor of love.

After I reach a place where I can get a truck to the deer, I load up the buck and take him to be checked in and weighed. In New England, this is typically a local store. This is a fun part of the experience. It is a good time to call your buddies and brag a little. Be sure to buy something from the folks operating the store where the tagging station is located and thank them. If there is a state biologist on hand, be sure to give them whatever information they need. It will only serve to help the herd.

Some people make the mistake of driving around with the buck for days to show him off, letting the sun hit him and not taking care of the meat. Depending on where I am and what the ambient temperature is, I might let the buck stay in my truck for one night at the most. I take care to prop the carcass open to cool, and then I try to get the deer hanging where it can really cool down. A shaded area with a breeze will work just fine, especially if it is cool at night. Hanging in Dad's garage works well for us, he has running water so the cavity and any blood shot areas can be rinsed and patted dry. You don't want to leave the meat wet. Ideally I let the buck hang for around ten to fourteen days if the temperatures are right. However, we've processed a deer in as quickly as two days after it was shot. Rigor mortis needs to pass before you cut the deer up. This takes about 24 hours. After that, the longer the buck hangs in 35-40° temperatures the more tender it becomes. If you have a meat locker available to you that can control temperature and humidity, hanging for two weeks and even up to four will yield high quality meat. I try to leave the skin on so the meat doesn't dry out, though this needs to be done thoughtfully as the skin, fat and hair act as insulators as well. These are just a few of the variables that go into the decision making process for hanging. You'll need to find what works for you based on your situation.

Dad is a butcher by trade so we process deer ourselves. There are many manuals on how to break a deer down. I tend to favor a division of a few roasts from the front end, some stew meat, burger and then the rest as steaks. I cut the steaks about an inch thick. We cut and wrap the backstraps in longer pieces so that they can be cooked whole and then sliced. We try to trim most of the fat, but depending on the flavor of an individual buck, we have also used that fat when grinding burger. Packages are made in meal sized portions, wrapped tightly in plastic wrap and then again in butcher paper. People seem to do well using a vacuum

Dad and I processing a deer for the freezer.

sealer but I haven't tried one yet. In either case, air is the enemy of frozen meat. If I have a particular cut I want is set aside for a specific recipe, I set the package aside and label it. With this approach, we have quality meat in the freezer from a deer for a year or even longer. Dad does some canning in a pressure canner and that is another good way of preserving venison.

It is important to learn a variety of ways to cook your venison. It is great to get creative with recipes, especially if you are new to cooking venison or if you are sharing with people who are new to eating it. What you can get away with at camp for a bunch of hungry hunters may not be as palatable at home. I recommend folks look up people like Hank Shaw and Steven Rinella for a lot of information regarding handling, butchering and quality recipes for venison and other game meats. The most common mistake people make with venison is overcooking it. Most

A full freezer is a nice result of the hunting season. Note the canned venison above.

cuts should be served medium rare. Find a good wine or beer to pair with your venison steak, put together a small green salad and cook some wild rice to go with it. You'll be eating like royalty.

Chapter 12

DRAGGING HOME

I love dragging a buck out of the woods. The exhilaration is not quite
the same as the moment you get him in your sights after a long, challenging chase, nor is it the same feeling of reverence as you wrap your
hands around those antlers for the first time. The long, slow burn of the
drag is a form of payment. The breaks it requires allow for reflection on
the hunt. The drag is the final chapter of the story. I like dragging because somewhere in the middle, I finish earning this buck and I start the
effort toward earning my next buck. I never know how much effort I will
have to put in, they are all different. Tracking requires simple payment
in sweat and hard work.

It is through desire, discipline and determination that we become successful trackers. You have to want that buck more than you want your
comfy bed or the heater in your truck. You have to want to track him
more than you want to find an easier way to shoot a deer. You have to
show up to hunt every day and put the work in – likely harder work than
what's required by the job you are on vacation from. You also need to
put the work in before the season to have every other possible variable
covered so that all you have to do is find him, catch him and get a bullet
in him. Lastly, you have to stay after it. When the track turns uphill
near the end of the day, headed away from the truck, what will you do?

Stay after him.

I feel a glow of accomplishment after I track a buck and drag him out
to the truck. The drive back to civilization gives me time to reflect and

ponder the place of hunting in my life and in society at large. Usually quite tired by this point in a long day, I feel stripped down physically and emotionally. The life and death struggle that we are all part of seems closer to the surface- even palpable. Personally, hunting has provided me with many things. Food, for one. Adventures, relationships and experiences. Deeper than that, it has also put me in touch with who I am and shown me, at least partly, my place in the world. Meaning. I think the things tracking deer has taught me have relevance in society at large. These are things I think about in the offseason as well. It is essential for hunters to give something back to the community and environment that enrich our lives so deeply. I would not be the same person if it were not for hunting. It has provided me with food for my body and my soul. It has opened up the world to me. Because of this, it is important to go beyond the simple purchase of a license. Hunters should become involved in protecting the environment that our quarry lives in. We are the original conservationists. Our great-grandfathers, in the midst of the depression, felt strongly enough about preserving our heritage and the land that they agreed to an excise tax on all hunting equipment. That money is used by all manner of fish and wildlife departments across the country.

Hunters should do more than be beneficiaries of the ideas of forward thinking people, we should contribute to their legacy. Follow the lead of people like Theodore Roosevelt, who protected our wildlife from commercially-driven extinction and set up our system of public lands. Consider the long term thinking of Nevada Senator Key Pittman and Virginia Congressman Absalom Willis Robertson who sponsored the Federal Aid in Wildlife Restoration Act of 1937 that pays for habitat and wildlife management to this day. As hunters, we need to continue the legacy that has restored wildlife populations across North America. We need to protect, maintain and grow the lands that sustain us and our way of life. The ability to manage these lands and animals for the good of the citizens was one of the key reasons our country's forefathers fled from England and the inability to hunt the King's deer. This is still important in today's society. We also need to share our experiences and introduce new people to the world of hunting so that it remains a viable activity and not one that fades into obscurity, or worse, is seen as unnecessary to the point it is not allowed.

While national concerns regarding conservation, access and preservation of federally managed land often dominate discussions, we need to look locally. The forested northern areas that trackers typically call home are made up of large tracts of uninhabited timber. In the West these tracts are often U.S. Forest Service land. As we look east, we encounter a changing ownership profile. There is the Superior National Forest in Minnesota, with some timber company land on its southern edge, and then Wisconsin and Michigan have a more even mix of public and private land. Get into NY and it is mostly state-owned forest, including the large uncut Adirondack State Park. Finally we arrive in New England, where the relatively small Green and White Mountain national forests provide some access for hunters. But the bulk of big woods hunting occurs on privately owned timber company lands, with tradition, easements and tax incentives facilitating hunter access. In the changing timber market, I am nervous about the long term prospect of these lands being managed in the same way. There are examples of public-private cooperation that may show us a way forward, with the benefit of continued recreational access coexisting with conservation and managed timber harvest.

One example exists here in my little corner of Vermont. The Kingdom Heritage Lands are part of a larger ecosystem known as the Northern Forest Lands that extend from NY to eastern Canada. Public access to these acres is protected through the collaboration of the US Fish and Wildlife Service, the State of VT, as well as non-profit and private interests that demonstrate the ability for multiple partners to work together.

When Champion International sold 132,000 acres in VT's Northeast Kingdom in 1998, a number of benefactors came together to protect and preserve this rich, multi-use area. Ecologically significant areas were divided into federally managed land, as part of the Silvio O. Conte National Wildlife Refuge, and state land as the West Mountain Wildlife Management Area. The remaining acreage was sold to a private timber company for working forestry with easements protecting certain natural resources and guaranteeing perpetual public access, even with future sales.

A variety of habitats exist across an extensive area of northern lowland forest and wetlands, ringed by hills and mountains of moderate elevation, drained by numerous streams flowing into the Connecticut River. This working landscape provides much needed room in wild places.

Politics can seem like an uphill drag for a hunter who values quiet and solitude. Much like dragging a buck out is a form of payment, so too is involvement on issues surrounding habitat conservation policy and stewardship. With these large scale problems shrouded in government bureaucracy and influenced by countless interest groups it seems reasonable to ask "What can I do?" Start with small simple answers.

Bring someone new out hunting and fishing.

Then write and call your politicians so they know where you stand. Talk to them about issues that are important to you. Start locally with your state Representatives and Senators. Speak up and make your voice heard. Get out and vote as well. Evaluate each candidate on issues and not simply party affiliation. Bring attention to your governor and national leaders, both those who are voted in and those who are appointed. Talk to local biologists and land managers; let them know you want to be involved.

If possible, contribute financially to outdoors organizations that support issues important to hunters. Far beyond just the Second Amendment, hunters also need to protect the land and the animals upon it.

Act ethically and responsibly. Treat the land, the animals and each other with respect. At a trailhead, give each other space to roam. If someone beats you to "your spot" that means you go elsewhere. Rather than bickering among ourselves on personal and philosophical issues, hunters need to present a united front against those who would like to see our heritage disappear. Demonstrate proper behavior in front of those who don't hunt. Ultimately the 80% of people who don't hunt but view it favorably for the purpose of obtaining meat will determine our fate. Being thoughtful about what we say, how we respect our quarry, how we respect the land and how we follow the rules will keep people on our side. Speak intelligently to those people who don't hunt. Share the value of your experiences for your soul in addition to the meat in your freezer. Connect with people emotionally as well as on a logical level. For too long hunters have hidden behind game management and meat for our freezer justifications, but we all know there is so much more to it. Rather than simply being anti the anti-hunters, be pro- something. Pro-experience, pro-adventure, pro-hunting.

Lastly, get out and track your buck. Enjoy the adventure and challenge. Tell your story. Share the lessons you've learned along the way.

It is only failure if you stop trying.

Chapter 13

ONE MORE FOR THE ROAD- EPILOGUE

THE arc of a hunting career for a dedicated deer tracker travels a long and winding road; one of much adventure and many unexpected experiences. Along the way there are a lot of twists and turns that should be thought of as learning opportunities. Just when I start to think I have it figured out, there's another curve, pothole or hill. None of us know just how many seasons we have, so each one is special, just as each buck we get to follow is special. But once in a while one stands out.

Big bucks sometimes seem to take on an almost mythical status. First of all they are rare and hard to find. Secondly, a lifetime of eluding predators of all types makes them hard to hunt. I believe individual personality traits are what allow these bucks to grow older and that those traits make them challenging to kill; things like where they choose to bed, when they like to move, and how they travel across the landscape. Lastly, the vast expanse of wilderness and often steep terrain where they live elevates the level of effort required to chase them. When I locate a buck that takes on these nearly magical qualities, he begins to haunt me.

During a couple of early season trips to NH in 2017 I had found evidence of a really good buck in one particular area and had started to piece together what I felt was his home range. Saturday before Thanksgiving I had traveled to this area because there was good snow. I managed to cut his track late in the day. I kept the pace up, trying to make up time with waning daylight and was able to jump him but not get a shot. I saw a lot of aggressive scrapes and rubs in the short time I chased him and knew he was interested in the doe groups nearby. Dad and I decided to head to this area of NH for our traditional Thanksgiving week hunting trip. The decision was made easier because the snow forecast was a little sketchy for the general region of Maine where we normally spend our vacation. With continued snow in the forecast I was hoping to find his fresh track again.

Monday was spent double-teaming on the track of a nice buck on the far edge of where I thought this buck roamed. We had taken a medium sized buck track to start the day and crossed the trail of a bigger buck. Though his track was older, we switched to the larger buck track. In two hours we had a much fresher track underfoot. He had caught up to a doe and was staying with her. He chased her into, over and under a bunch of blown down softwood. They split away from the other deer down low and headed uphill. Dad and I split up along the mountain top, suspecting the two deer would be in front of us somewhere. I moved north along the eastern edge of the mountain and Dad swung a little west toward a clear-cut. I stayed with the track and came across his very fresh track made in the snow warmed by the mid-day sun. Twenty minutes of easing along and the doe jumped up below me at 50 yards. I couldn't see the buck. She ran off to the north and as she entered a patch of softwood, the buck was behind her. He had been hidden by a patch of timber. Two hours of chasing ensued and when the day was done, Dad had seen a piece of him in the distance one other time but no shots were fired. It was the start of a good week.

The next couple days were taken up searching for good buck tracks. I followed one buck for two and a half miles and when he crossed a road, someone else had started following him. That was a disappointing turn of events, but it happens when a buck is covering a lot of ground. I took a long loop back to the truck to explore some different territory and get a feel for the lay of the land. Finally on Thursday I again found the track of the big fella, but it was high in a mountain pass and was two days old. I at least knew he was around. Friday I searched again for his track, getting picky on how I chose to expend my effort. I got back to my truck that afternoon and found a note on my seat from Dad that he had tracked a buck and shot him. I drove to where I knew he had been parked and he was there waiting with the first buck he tracked and shot all by himself!

The following morning I was on my own. My plan was to swing up onto a couple of small peaks and check the saddles between them. I knew this area held a couple of doe groups within the buck's range and connected several of his signpost rubs. I was hoping to cut his track. An hour into the day, I finally crossed his path from the night before. Warming temperatures through the day and melting snow made determining the age easy, but meant I had snow that was going to disappear. With a skiff of snow in the track, blurred edges and a frozen bottom, the track was from the night before. His tracks crossed a saddle that I had chased him through two weeks before and headed up another knob above a clear-cut and near a signpost rub he had hit earlier in the season. I kept the pace up as I moved along the older track. He crossed his own even older tracks and I saw boot prints that suggested he had been chased by a hunter the day before. The buck's track finally peeled away and I could see where he had encountered a doe and her fawn. I spent the next hour sorting out where he had chased them around. There was evidence of the group feeding heavily on ferns and old man's beard on blown down trees, with several beds located in the midst of all of it. I finally found where they had left the slope that they had been on through the night. I promptly found the now-empty beds of the buck and doe that I had jumped while I was following their wanderings. His bed was significantly larger and had tarsal stains in it, with the accompanying stink still hanging in the air.

I now had a big buck jumped up and a fresh track laid out ahead of me. I waited 20 minutes, had a snack and a drink of water and then started at an easy pace along the track. He circled the mountain back toward the north, where I'd originally cut his track, but up higher. In short order I encountered two bull moose who were moving through ahead of me. I didn't want to scare them and then have them spook the buck, so I let them meander away about 100 yards ahead of me until the deer's tracks diverged from the moose's path. The tracks swung uphill, still running. Reaching a bench on the mountainside, the deer started to slow to walk and turned 180° to head south. With the sun in my eyes, I slowed my pace as the tracks led me into a spruce top.

The buck's track was quite distinct; obviously larger and the imprint of his rear left foot had an extra-long outside toe that stuck out a little. I only had to glance down to know I was following his movements. The deer calmed down and began to meander. The doe went back to feeding, drifting around some blown over trees. At this point the buck split away from her, drifting toward the east. I tiptoed around blowdowns and tried to slide through the brush silently. Slowly cruising over the bumps and hollows along the top of this mountain, the buck's track began to pitch downhill.

The track was traveling to the right, angling across the slope. I glanced ahead along the track. When I looked left down the steepening angle of the mountain suddenly there he was, appearing as if he was a ghost. 70 yards away I could see his dark brown coat against the snow. Standing broadside to me, but facing to the right, he must have switchbacked down the hill. His square body was obviously large. His head was turned to look at me, hidden slightly in the hardwood growth behind him. Quickly I pulled up my rifle and looked to confirm that it was the buck I was tracking. Seeing the outline of his substantial rack, I lowered the crosshairs toward his body. At the same time, he gathered himself to bolt. I shot and worked the pump as he accelerated to full speed. Another shot. He disappeared. I ran to the ridgeline above where he had run hoping to see him. There was no sign of him.

I took a deep breath and switched out the magazine in my rifle. I replayed things in my mind. It had been quick, but felt tentatively successful. I marked my location with the GPS and noted the compass bearing that would take me in the direction of where the buck had been standing. A sip of water only helped my dry mouth a little. I abandoned the track and made my way down to where the buck had been standing.

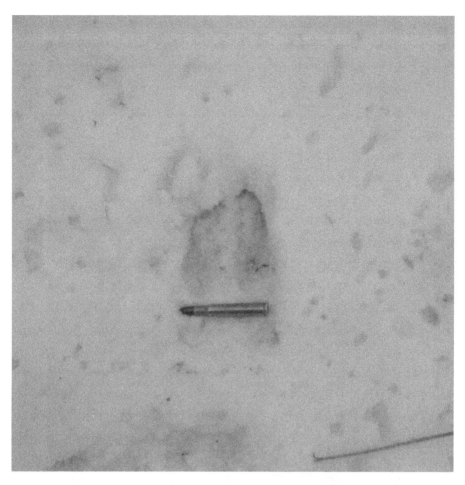

Track of the New Hampshire buck that will haunt me for years to come.

I got there and found nothing. Not even a track. Had he actually been a ghost?

Further searching revealed he had been back a little in the tree line. His track showed where he was standing and where he took off. No hair, no blood. My stomach turned and I squatted there in disbelief. I took up the track again and followed him down into a clear-cut, through a thick swamp and then back up the mountain. He circled the top and then crossed into his old tracks from the night before. The midday sun was causing the snow to drip out of the trees and on the south facing slopes it was melting away completely. Two and a half hours after shooting at him, I finally lost his track. I started back to the truck for the ride back to Vermont feeling ill about my failed opportunity.

A week's worth of effort had culminated in a miss; I was in a bad state of mind. When the goal is to track and kill a buck over 200 pounds it is hard to be consoled by the idea that everything went right except for that final, and essential, step. To have it be derailed by poor shooting, regardless of the speed or challenge of the situation, seemed irrelevant. I talked to Dad and my buddy Ben that night. We debated possible causes. I shot my rifle- it was dialed in perfect. Buck fever? Maybe, but I felt like my head was right during the encounter. To put it simply, I choked. I think that perhaps my timing was off. As I pulled down from his head toward his vitals he may have started to drop to take off and seeing this, I may have pulled the trigger a split second too early, causing a miss over his back.

I felt emotionally raw for the next couple of days. The level of physical exertion, mental fatigue and disappointment left me wrung out like an old dish rag. Chances like that are exceedingly rare. I was lucky to have encountered him. I have learned that moving on from a miss is important to regaining confidence. Hunters who track are going to miss shots. Much like getting back on the proverbial horse, it is important to find another buck to track. A tracker should start each day with a renewed mindset and when the snow is good, a mind fully focused on killing the buck in front of him. Trust me; you'll have the whole winter to contemplate all the things that didn't go right.

It took some time to begin to see the growth that was possible from this failure. All was not lost. I started to formulate a plan to rectify the things that went wrong. I'll do more shooting in the next year that focuses on tracking-specific scenarios. There will be more work at multiple shot angles and even faster target acquisition. I will do more scouting to find bucks like this one. My love of tracking deer was also reaffirmed; as devastated as I felt, I also had a deep sense of exhilaration from finding and tracking a buck of that caliber.

That buck is still roaming the woods. He'll forever roam my mind along with all the other bucks from the close calls I've had. With the road to the next season rolled out in front of me, I am pleasantly haunted by the memories of bucks that got away. Each step I learn a little more. Nine months from now, if he makes it through the winter and the conditions are right, I might be lucky enough to cross his track.

Recommended Reading

Big Woods Bucks (Vol 1 and 2) by Hal Blood

How to Bag the Biggest Buck of Your Life by Larry Benoit

Big Bucks the Benoit Way by Bryce Towsley

Adirondack Deer Trackers: Stories as Told in Deer Camp by DiNitto, Grabowski, Massett, Williams

Omnivores Dilemma by Michael Pollan

Bloodties: Nature, Culture, and the Hunt by Ted Kerasote

A Sand County Almanac by Aldo Leupold

Buck, Buck, Moose by Hank Shaw

The Complete Guide to Hunting, Butchering, and Cooking Wild Game: Vol 1: Big Game by Steven Rinella

ABOUT THE AUTHOR

MATT Breton is a hunter, writer, physical therapist and U.S. Army veteran. While his first love is tracking deer in New England, Matt loves to pursue a variety of critters across North America's public lands, including elk, mule deer, snowshoe hare, grouse and trout. His Outdoor Athlete column appeared monthly in the *Northwoods Sporting Journal* for several years and he has had work published nationally in *Fur Fish Game* and *Backcountry Journal,* as well as numerous articles online as a team member of Big Woods Bucks. Keep up with him at www.matthewbreton.com.

CPSIA information can be obtained
at www.ICGtesting.com
Printed in the USA
LVHW110631201222
735543LV00004B/606